The Culture War in America

A Society in Chaos

by Bob Rosio

Huntington House Publishers

Huntington House Publishers
P.O. Box 53788
Lafayette, Louisiana 70505

Library of Congress Card Catalog Number 95-77033
ISBN 1-56384-097-9

Printed in the U.S.A.

To Marie, my wife
To Patty, my typist
To George, my printer
To Gerald, my computer guy

Contents

1

Living on the Edge of the Volcano

History often seems to repeat itself. There are two good reasons for this. First, all history is a variation on a theme, an outworking of the cosmic conflict which began with Satan's expulsion from the highest heaven. When Satan's theater of operations switched to planet earth, evil invaded the Garden of Eden. On one hand, the God of grace and truth has continually reached out throughout history to a lost and confused mankind with the intention of saving men and women from the power of sin, of self, and of Satan. On the other hand, Satan and his followers have continued their rebellion against a holy God and have sought to influence others to do the same. There are no neutrals in this conflict.

The second reason is that unregenerate man (influenced by selfishness) unwisely tends to make the same mistakes over and over, generation after generation. The reason for this failure is that true wisdom and knowledge begin with the reverential fear of the Lord God. Satan is a master of deception and destruction. Deception leads to destruction. The most effective type of deception is self-deception, and people are most likely to be deceived where they most wish to be deceived—at the point of pride and selfishness. The only antidote for deception (and the only protection from destruction) is a receptivity toward God's truth (2 Thess. 2:10). This receptivity usually requires some reorientation and reprioritizing, for by nature God's ways are not our ways.

The ancient city of Pompeii is unique in world history. It was buried in the volcanic eruption of Mount Vesuvius in A.D. 79 and remained entombed under the lava and volcanic ash for nineteen hundred years. It was accidentally rediscovered in 1760, and has provided a wealth of information on Roman life in the first century. The ancient Roman historians described Pompeii as a typical pleasure-loving resort city. Modern historical reconstruction has also shown it to be a city of selfish hedonistic frivolity, decadence and savagery—a pagan city whose inhabitants worshiped pagan gods and goddesses, a city perhaps not unlike some modern cities.

In August of A.D. 79 the inhabitants of Pompeii were living their lives as usual. They ignored the rumblings from nearby Mount Vesuvius, a mountain which some among them worshiped as holy. Although the dormant volcano had rumbled for as long as anyone could remember, it had never erupted. People had lived on its fertile slopes for centuries, creating and working prosperous farms and vineyards. A minor earthquake had occurred sixteen years earlier, causing some minor damage to the city of Pompeii. In response to the fears of the populace, the rulers of the city sent for an augur, a fortune teller who practiced divination through the reading of the entrails of a bird. The augur pronounced the city safe. In early August, however, some hidden underground changes affected the water supply to the city of Pompeii. The citizens of

Pompeii adjusted as best they could to the temporary inconvenience and sought to live their lives as usual, content to trust in their favorable augury.

On 24 August A.D. 79 the holy mountain called Vesuvius, which had never erupted, suddenly spewed forth poisonous clouds of thick, sulfuric smoke, and a veritable hail of hot cinders, lava, and volcanic ash. The citizens were caught by total surprise and most of them died instantly in the midst of their daily pursuits. The city of Pompeii disappeared from human history in one day, proving that a lack of knowledge can be dangerous, and can lead to destruction. This is true for both individuals and for societies.

While the most famous volcanic eruption in history was probably that of Vesuvius, many Americans may be more aware of the recent volcanic eruption of Mount St. Helens in the state of Washington. It, too, has some important lessons to teach. The citizens of Pompeii did not have the advantage of modern technology. They perished primarily through a lack of knowledge. American geologists had long monitored the volcanic activity at Mount St. Helens and predicted the potential dangers of the mounting pressure. At a certain point, the local population was advised to evacuate their homes. It was widely reported in our national newspapers that not everyone chose to heed the warning. An elderly gentleman, for whatever reason, refused to heed the warnings, entreaties, and supplications of the scientists, the law officers, and his friends and family. He was determined not to leave his home. He did not believe that "his mountain" would erupt. His charred remains were later discovered in the ruins of his home. Although he had the knowledge of the impending disaster at hand to guide him, it did not move him to act on the knowledge he had. A refusal to act on the available knowledge can also lead to destruction.

The volcano is clearly one of the most impressively destructive phenomena to be found in nature. A volcanic eruption is the sudden and violently destructive venting of pressure which is the result of the fiery bubbling and boiling of a deep subterranean cauldron. This gradual build-up of pressure is accompanied by certain indicators and warning signs which are obvious to a trained eye. The study of volcanoes and of volcanic activity is called volcanology. I suppose that in a sense, I am a spiritual volcanologist. I believe that our society is presently living on the edge of a volcano which is getting ready to erupt. Society, through lack of knowledge, or through disbelief or disobedience, is ignoring all the warning signs, the signs of impending disaster. My job is to warn the citizens of modern Pompeii (the secular humanists of today) of this impending disaster and to urge people to make wise decisions, decisions that will lead to salvation.

A syndrome is a group of signs and symptoms that occur together and which characterize a particular abnormality. From God's point of view, it is abnormal to refuse to believe His warnings of impending judgment. The refusal to accept God's offer of salvation is what I call the Noah syndrome. Noah preached God's Word to an indifferent audience for 120 years, but he had no success outside his own immediate family. Just as the citizens of Pompeii had never seen a volcanic eruption, earth-dwellers in Noah's time had never seen a flood. Thus, they did not believe that Noah's message could possibly be correct. For most people, seeing is believing. With God, believing is seeing. Because Noah's contemporaries had no relationship with God, His Word seemed like foolishness to them. Their foolish hearts had been darkened by the terminal disease of selfishness. They were a people who were in love with sin. They were also a people who rejected every warning from God.

The Bible clearly states that at the end of this age, people will be as they were in the time of Noah, ignoring and rejecting God in order to pursue their own selfish and sinful interests. I believe that we are now living in that prophesied time period. People are increasingly both accepting and promoting sin, calling good evil and evil good. They reject the idea that God judges sin, thus mocking His Word. Like Sodom and Gomorrah, they have lost the most basic comprehension of common decency and morality. They have lost the ability to blush over sin. God's Word declares such a society to be terminal. God's first judgment came in a flood. The next judgment will come in fire.

The Spirit of Truth is working on the hearts of people all over the world—convicting them of sin, righteousness, and judgment. He is opening and softening hearts toward God's truth. He is preparing His church to minister His saving truth to a world in peril. The options of mankind are the same as they ever were—to accept God's truth and live, or to reject God's truth and perish. "When truth retreats, tyranny advances. And in American life today, truth is retreating, and tyranny is advancing."[1] Francis Schaeffer said, "The crisis is one of truth, and if we lose, we will have tyranny in America before the end of this century."[2] That is what this book is about. That is also primarily what the culture war is about: the battle for truth.

2

The Kulturkampf

When I was a young boy, I was quite fascinated by ants. Ants seemed to me to live such organized, busy, and purposeful lives! By dint of daily exploration and observation (as young boys are prone to do), my friends and I had duly noted and recorded the existence of two prominent anthills in our neighborhood. One colony of ants was black and the other red. The anthills provided us with frequent entertainment in the hot summer months. (This was before television gripped the national soul.)

Since the ant colonies were located a half block from each other, we assumed that each was unaware of the existence of the other ant community. One day, however, the red ants surged out of their redoubt, went a half block in a straight and militarylike line, took a sharp right turn, and attacked the black ant colony. I can't imagine how the red ants had discovered the black ants, but there could be no doubt that it was their intention to destroy their distant neighbors. I understood, even as a very young boy, that by some immutable law of nature, black ants and red ants are incompatible. What I was witnessing in nature was one of the most cherished philosophies of modern humanistic man: Darwinism. Aided by hatred and technology, Darwinism was put into its most terrible applications by Hitler's Nazis. Hitler felt that what was good for ants would be even better for human beings. Hitler believed strongly in the survival of the fittest. He also believed that he would determine who was fit to survive. Hitler would have recognized the battle to the death between the black ants and the red ants as a "Kulturkampf."

Hitler understood the Kulturkampf ("Culture Struggle") to be one of the guiding principles of human existence. His Kulturkampf was based upon a spiritual principle which endorsed a fight to the death between nazism and any other system of thought or belief which stood in its way. The Nazis were playing for large stakes: global domination. They believed that their final victory would occur only when they had successfully imposed their version of culture upon the rest of the world. Hitler called it "the molding of the will." The German philosopher Hegel referred to it as "universality of thought." This worldwide universality of thought was to be achieved by a combination of reeducation and brutality. Hitler strongly believed that he had been providentially called to introduce a new age into world history. His new age was to be based upon a new culture. This is still the goal of the New Age movement.

In the West, the word *culture* is loosely synonymous with our concept of civilization itself. Our culture is the sum total of all that has shaped us. It involves what we believe, how we live, what we hold as sacred and precious, and what we hope to become. It is important for people to realize that nazism was a spiritual system that was translated into a terrible political reality. It is also important to understand that nazism was not simply a historical aberration. It was a carefully planned assault on the great traditions of the

Western world. It was a rejection of the entire historical flow of Western civilization. Specifically, it was a
rejection of the Judeo-Christian ethic and a return to
barbaric paganism. The spiritual forces which were
behind nazism did not disappear once Hitler was de-
feated. They have continued to work like an evil leaven
in our society.

Our society is once again involved in a Kulturkampf.
The winner of this culture war will determine the direction civilization will take in the coming years. Although the outcome of this culture war will ultimately
affect the life of every single person on the earth,
relatively few people even seem aware of its existence.
There are those, of course, who are more or less aware
of its existence, but who do not choose to get involved
in this escalating struggle. One day, however, they will
sadly discover that there are no neutrals in this war.
Don Feder said that "in the culture war, only one side
will triumph. Someone's values will be written into law,
taught in the public schools, and validated by the culture."[1] Lynn Stanley wrote that "there are two camps
at war in this battle for the heart and soul of America.
In one camp there are those who believe in moral
absolutes; in the other are those who do not." (To
those who think rationally, the argument is moot because humanists say there are "absolutely" no absolutes!) "As battle lines are drawn, those who win the
cultural war will win the mind and conscience of this
nation and, thus, chart its course toward greatness or
destruction."[2]

Nazism was a demonic intrusion into history. It
caused the regression of an entire nation to a sub-
civilizational level, to a time of blood thirsty pagan
barbarism. It was also a clear illustration of C. S. Lewis'
belief that civilization is a rarity, attained with difficulty
and easily lost. Lewis believed that man's natural state
(if left to his own devices) is barbarism. He did not
share the optimistic belief of modern psychology (and

of the New Age movement) that man is by nature an infinitely perfectible being, an autonomous creature of boundless potential. Donald Grey Barnhouse said that degeneration is the law of all life apart from God. The second law of thermodynamics, which teaches that the universe is wearing out and running down, has both a physical and a spiritual application. Scripture instructs us that righteousness exalts a nation and that sin is a disgrace for any people. Oswald Chambers said that "The disposition of sin is not immorality and wrong doing, but the disposition of self-realization—that I am my own god. Sin is not wrong doing, it is wrong being—deliberate and emphatic independence of God."[3]

It is also the essence of secular humanism. The mandatory condition for righteousness, both for individuals and for nations, is a submission to God; for true righteousness stems from a right relationship with God. When Germany rejected God's truth, it also rejected God Himself. The spirit that influenced Germany to embrace deception is now moving again in our own age and in our own society. Germany was a historical and prophetic signpost, a spiritual microcosm. The deception and destruction that were orchestrated in Germany will soon be seen again on the planet earth in the dreadful ministry of the horsemen in Revelation 6. I do not simply believe that what happened in Germany could happen again. I believe that it is already happening.

It has been said that the first casualty in every war is truth. That is most certainly the case in the current culture war. In my book, *The Satanization of Society*, I examined the ongoing and systematic elimination of God's truth from our society and the substitution of a secular humanistic belief system. Unchecked secular humanism (the dethroning of God and the deification of man) always leads to demonism. Secular humanism and demonism have in common that they are both types of rebellion against God.

Jude (verse 11) speaks of "the way of Cain." The way of Cain is the way of willful rebellion against God, the way that leads from deception to destruction. Cain is the spiritual father of all those throughout history who have rejected God's truth in order to do things their own way. By rejecting God's truth, Cain also rejected a relationship with God. Cain rejected God's truth in order to construct a belief system more to his liking.

There is a mountain ridge in the Rocky Mountains which forms a natural dividing point. This watershed separates the rivers flowing in an easterly direction from those flowing in a westerly direction. These rivers have a common origin, but they have different destinations. Jesus Christ is the great dividing point in history. Those who love the truth flow toward Him. Those who do not love the truth flow away from Him. Christ Jesus is both the source and goal of history, and eventually every member of the human race will be forced to deal with the truth that Christ Jesus personifies. It may be sooner, or it may be later, but it will most assuredly happen. The present culture war is being waged along the dividing line of God's truth.

I recently was a guest on a radio talk show from California. After my first book, *Hitler and the New Age*, appeared, I did well over a hundred radio shows on it. About half of the shows were on Christian stations, half on secular stations. I found almost all of them to be quite interesting, but I found this particular show to be especially significant. The host of this talk show went to great pains to let me know that he was hostile to my Christian position, proudly proclaiming that he was a neo-pagan. Just for fun, I asked him to explain to me exactly what it was that he worshiped. He stumbled around, and although there were lots of "er's" and "well ah's" in his explanation, he was unable to explain to me what he worshiped. In essence, the simple truth was that he worshiped himself.

It may seem chic to some to be a neo-pagan. Neo-pagans are not very different from pagans anywhere at any time in human history. I didn't find this particular neo-pagan talk show host very convincing (although I am sure he is in some ways typical). Christians are believers. They know what they believe and why they believe it. My neo-pagan talk show host seemed to me to be too lazy (or too intellectually dishonest) to formulate what he believed in such a way that he could explain it. At any rate, I am sure that if he could not explain it, he could also not actually live it. True discipleship is hard work.

Idolatry is at the core of all paganism. Its bottom line is that it is a rejection of the true and living God in order to worship a less demanding god of one's own choosing. It may be Mother Earth, the forces of nature, demonic nature gods, a physical object (either natural or manmade), or even the worship of self. We live in a time and a place where idolatrous self-worship reigns supreme.

The radical feminist and ecological movements, which are so dear to the politically correct crowd, are also paganistic movements. They unite paganistic concepts like witchcraft, goddess worship, and animism/polytheism/pantheism.

All occult involvement is also a type of paganism. Those who turn to Ouija boards, tarot cards, fortune-telling, horoscopes, psychics, channeling, seances, Edgar Cayce, and so forth are involved with satanic deception—a deception that could lead to terrible destruction—both spiritual and physical. These people may well be sincere and convinced that their motives are right. God, however, judges both motives and methods by the light of His Word. In that light, all those who practice paganism stand condemned. Many people reject Christianity because they find it restrictive. They got that part right, anyway. It is restrictive in the sense that it puts limits on what people can do. According to those who worship at the altar of the sovereign self (a major entry point into the kingdom of Satan), it deprives people of "freedom." It does deprive people of the freedom to sin without consequences. The road to maturity and sanity is built upon responsibility and accountability. I recently saw a bumper sticker that said, "How much can I get away with and still be a Christian?" Unfortunately, that sums up the mindset of many of those who currently claim the name of Christ. My bumper sticker answer to that question would be a simple "Jesus is Lord."

At any rate, my dialogue with the self-proclaimed neo-pagan radio host in California sparked a succession of hostile New Agers to call in.

In the main they were quite angry at my outrageous Christian views. I, however, found their views quite informative. In the final analysis, while they rejected the God that I worship and the truth which I hold as dear and sacred, the best that they could offer as a substitute was the worship of themselves, the creation, false gods, or their own sin. It reminded me of Jeremiah's description of those who pursued emptiness and became empty themselves (Jer. 2:5). We see in that condition of emptiness the core condition of the New Age movement. All the New Age callers had in common is that they rejected the idea of God's absolute truth, choosing instead to believe lies that were to their liking. Despite what they chose to believe, God's truth is absolute, universal, eternal—and personal. To reject God's truth is to reject God Himself. The rejection of God's truth is the essence of the current Kulturkampf.

During the course of the conversation (which went on for over two hours) I believe that the term "Christian Right" must have been mentioned about fifty times. It was not a political term for these callers but a pejo-

rative one. Many of those who called were committed
to the idea that the Christians are the true Nazis in
America, revealing a terrible darkness in their hearts,
as well as a colossal ignorance of American history.
They became enraged when I suggested that they were
involved with idolatry, giving me the tiniest appreciation of the terrible wrath that was directed at the friends
of Daniel when they refused to worship the image of
Nebuchadnezzar, causing the arrogant monarch to
throw a tantrum. They were especially incensed at three
things. The first was my suggestion that Hitler and
nazism had occult roots. The second thing that seemed
to enrage them was that Christians dare to run for
public office. I made an effort to explain to them that
such things are natural in a democracy. Witches can
run for office. Neo-pagans can. Even Christians can.

The third thing that infuriated them was that Christians have their own radio and television stations and
shows. I believe that the existence of Christian media
guarantees that the voice of truth cannot be totally
extinguished in our society. The current media stance
in America can be demonstrated by various criteria.
The first would be to judge their intention by their
own silence regarding authentic Christianity. The secular media is of course very noisy when it comes to
Christian scandal (the disgrace of Christian public fig-
ures) and in the analyses of events like the attack upon
David Koresh's group, Jim Jones, and so forth. The
stance of the entertainment media is one of open hostility. Christians are usually mocked as fanatical bigots
and oddballs, hopelessly at odds with twentieth-century
modernity. At the same time, there has been a great
increase in programming of both occult subjects and
of humanistic Christian views (a specialty of PBS). I
studiously avoid the latter unless I specifically want to
monitor the humanistic views on Christ and Christianity. I recently caught a short segment on the life and

times of Jesus. The narrator suggested the possibility that Jesus may have learned a lot from the preaching of John the Baptist, and that, in fact, He may even have picked up some of His preaching style and content from John. How sadly absurd! But, that is exactly why Christian media exists—to tell the truth. The true desire of the secular humanist elite is to eliminate the influence of Christianity in politics (as is already the case in American education) and in the public forum. That approach is not new. It was employed most efficiently and effectively by Hitler in Germany, Stalin in the Soviet Union, and Mao in China. All three tyrants were used by Satan to establish kingdoms of darkness, kingdoms which rejected God's light. The sum total of the fruits of misery caused by these servants of darkness will only truly be understood in heaven.

The antichrist spirit always works to attack God's truth. It is always one of the primary interests of those who are filled with that spirit to attack and suppress God's Word in society. The Book of Ephesians calls them "children of wrath and darkness." Their darkness is internal. It is in that significant fact that the sworn enemies of the Christian message manifest the legacy of Hitler, Stalin, and Mao. It is also a sobering look at the bottom line of the politically correct agenda of the New Age movement. They are working to destroy the Judeo-Christian ethic, to erase this ethic from the memory banks of society, to eradicate its cultural heritage, and to introduce a new age of Satanic barbarism into world history.

The current Kulturkampf is the terminal conflict between truth and error. In every war in the modern era, the accepted practice prior to an all-out assault upon enemy territory has been to "soften up" the enemy positions with a massive barrage of artillery fire, naval bombardment, or saturation bombing from the air. The entire world saw the effectiveness of this technique during the Gulf War. The allied military technology and firepower easily destroyed Saddam Hussein's military machine. The fierce and relentless allied bombardment also destroyed the infrastructure of the nation, effectively paralyzing it and depriving it of its ability to defend itself.

Similar things occur in a spiritual sense. When Satan bombards society with his own big guns, it is his intention to destroy the spiritual infrastructure of a society, preparing that society for his own all-out assault. This satanic barrage has been going on with increasing ferocity since the end of World War II. The softening-up process has had a terrible effect on the moral fiber and fabric of our society. It is time to sound the trumpet and mobilize for the final battles. There will be no neutrals in this war. No compromise will be possible. One of the great lessons of World War II was that it is not possible to compromise with evil. After Neville Chamberlain signed a pact of appeasement with Hitler in Munich, Winston Churchill delivered a prophetic indictment in the House of Commons concerning England's refusal to oppose evil; an indictment, which when seen in a spiritual sense and within the context of the present spiritual culture war, still gives a prophetic direction for the American church and for the nation at large: "And do not suppose this is the end. This is only the beginning of the reckoning. This is only the first sip, the first foretaste of a bitter cup which will be proffered to us year by year, unless, by a supreme recovery of moral health and martial vigor, we arise again and take our stand for freedom as in olden times."[4]

Don Wildmon put a modern twist on Churchill's words when he said that "we Americans are caught up in a great struggle unlike any which we have faced before. Our struggle is not with an enemy from beyond our shores as it has been in the past; it is being waged inside our very borders. The great struggle is one of values."[5] I call this struggle between those who hold irreconcilable values the culture war.

3

The Culture War

Since the Bible says that there is wisdom to be found in a multitude of godly counselors, I like to test an idea or two on my friends and colleagues from time to time. When I told several of them that I was working on a book on the culture war, they responded by asking me, "What culture war?" Although they were not familiar with the term, I found that as I explained it to them they were already very aware of the existence of the culture war. I was not surprised.

Christians are at least generally aware that history is a spiritual process. They are becoming even more aware as this fact is being worked out all around them on a daily basis, and as we are moving toward the end of the age. Although prophecy is being fulfilled by current events, spiritual things can still only be spiritually discerned by those who have an eye to see and understand what they are seeing. Those who don't, won't (unless, of course, God opens their eyes). In the meantime, much of what goes on will remain a mystery to most people. Although many people are still unaware that we are caught in a culture war, they are very aware of many of the individual battles which are being

fought within the context of the larger war. Don Feder
believes that Liberals hate the expression "culture war"
because it is far too revealing. In case you also are
unfamiliar with the term "culture war," the definition
is simple. Paul Schenck calls this struggle "America's
second Civil War."

> We are in the middle of the greatest ideological
> struggle in America's history. We who belong
> to the current generation ... are living in the
> midst of a very great conflict, indeed, a "com-
> bat" of personal and public convictions. It is no
> secret that this conflict has been brewing for
> some time. I am referring to the clash between
> two competing philosophies or ways of living.[1]

The culture war, however, is not simply a clash of
political ideals. The culture war is Satan's all-out effort
to remake society into his moral and ethical image. It
is his desire to produce a society which has been conditioned not only to reject truth and to embrace error,
but to actually hate the truth and to seek to suppress
and destroy it. Although the origin of the culture war
is spiritual, it is being contested in the physical realm,
for Satan uses people to establish his agenda. The bottom line of this agenda is his intention to reign over
the entire planet during the period which the Bible
identifies as the Great Tribulation. In this case, Satan
is using the secular humanist elite (in the government,
the courts, the media, and the academic establishment)
as agents of change and to shape public opinion. Much
of this book will deal with these specific areas and their
impact on the average American citizen. By government, I primarily mean the federal government. Gary
L. Bauer writes that most Americans are only now
beginning to realize how different the values of those
in Washington are from those of the average citizen.
He writes:

You believe that government is a limited instrument. Washington, D.C. believes that government can create a utopia on Earth. You believe in a thing called "truth." Washington, D.C. believes in the all-importance of moral relativism. You believe in the importance of faith, community, and family. Washington, D.C. believes in the all-importance of the state and the "new world order." You believe that America could once more be the shining "city on a hill" that its first settlers strove to build. Washington, D.C. believes that it is that city.[2]

By courts, I mean the entire humanistic judiciary, but I will give special attention to the Supreme Court. By media, I mean both the news and the entertainment media. By schools, I mean primarily the government financed and controlled schools (from nursery school to high school all the way through the politically correct American colleges and universities). I do not believe that these agents of change represent the views held by the majority of Americans. They do not represent the people. Their plan is to control from above and from within. To a large degree, the culture war is the war which is being waged by the American elites against American culture, against the things which Americans have traditionally held to be precious and sacred. Prof. Philip Rieff warned, "The rot always begins at the top meaning that societies fall from the faults of the elites, not from the shortcomings of those at the bottom."[3]

There are two primary classifications of elites in America. They have in common the pursuit, maintenance, and use of power. The first group (the core of the New Age movement) concerns itself with spiritual power, although they are also very interested in the secular corridors to power: government, education, the courts, the media. The second group is what Dr. Charles

Murray has called "the cognitive elite." They are the politicians, lawyers, judges, professors, bureaucrats, journalists, etc., who generally have a liberal, leftist, socialist world view. They consider themselves superior, believing that they know best, that they should rule over and guide society toward a "progress" which is "being retarded by unqualified, amateurish citizens encumbered by retrograde, parochial values."[4]

They are America's patrician class. They are also easy prey for Satan. Blinded by pride and selfishness, they are being used to contribute to the disintegration of society which will facilitate his eventual (and temporary) control over the human race.

> Just as Lenin had introduced the concept of a ruling elite of professional revolutionaries that would lead the workers of the world into communism, so the New Left today advances a platform clearly built on a ruling elite of intellectuals and professionals, e.g., professors, lawyers, and medical researchers, that will lead the American "middle class" and "underclass" into the false consensus. If the ordinary American does not consent to the secularist–New Left consensus, if many academics are to have their way, then the dissenter would be subject to ridicule, ostracism, expulsion, civil, and even criminal penalties, including jail.[5]

Their initial mission is to banish every vestige of the Judeo-Christian ethic from the public forum—to oppose it, to vilify it, and eventually to criminalize it, thus clearing the way for their New World Order ethic. This elite is composed of those who are deceivers, and those who are the deceived. The deceived and the deceivers have in common a rebellion against the God of the Bible. Some serve Satan directly. Some serve him indirectly by serving the false gods of humanism and selfishness. Humanism, however, will eventually be swallowed up by demonism in the reign of the Antichrist. The culture war is steadily moving our society to a crisis point, to a point of chaos. "The crisis is in the character of our culture, where the values that restrain inner vices and develop inner virtues are eroding. Unprincipled men and women, disdainful of their moral heritage and skeptical of Truth itself, are destroying our civilization by weakening the very pillars upon which it rests."[6]

The culture war will eventually profoundly touch the life of each American. Since this is true, Americans by the millions need to understand the source, substance, and significance of this struggle. Thomas Jefferson spoke to our current situation when he said that "you need not expect to remain both ignorant and free." In matters of liberty, ignorance is never bliss. In this war, Christians have one great advantage. He also believed that, "Christians are not confounded by arrogant" intellectual elitism that asserts that human existence is a meaningless event in an unending, mindless flow of meaningless events. They are unimpressed by the pompous, humanistic idea that we are born out of nothingness, to live and die, only to disappear back into nothingness.

"Christians know this kind of thinking makes absolutely no sense at all. They see this dark rhetoric for what it is: the verbal flailings of disoriented and frightened people who do not have philosophic handles on themselves or the universe in which they live."[7]

Satan's specialty is deception. It is the first step in his program. Satan works best in darkness. He has learned how to disguise his activities in order to be as effective as possible. The culture war was thus carried on for years more or less as a covert activity because mainstream America still held a Christian world view, cherishing things like responsibility, the work ethic, commitment, honesty, and godly morality. The essence of all occult things (both in matters spiritual and in matters political) is secrecy. The goal of those who have given themselves over to occult powers is to gain power: power over others, over their own lives, and over their environment.

Those who have been working to produce cultural change have worked like termites within the structure of our society. They have done their work diligently and effectively, eventually producing a cumulative effect. Their successes illustrate the thought of the philosopher David Hume who said that it is seldom that liberty of any kind is lost all at once. The price of liberty is indeed eternal vigilance based on a historical perspective. Although I don't suppose that there is ever a good war, there are sometimes good reasons to fight a war. The recent war in the Gulf might be one example. There were other wars in American history which were fought at least partially on principle. Until relatively recently, Americans believed that there actually were principles worth fighting for, and even worth dying for. The Revolutionary War would be an example of fighting for principles. Our Founding Fathers would be amazed and appalled over what we have done with the heritage they gave us, over what we now believe, and over what we have become. "The American Revolution was based on three observations. The first is that human beings are flawed and not to be trusted with too much power over their fellow humans, for they will surely abuse it." The others are that "there is no greater threat to human liberty than government," and that "no group of people was born (or elected) to lord it over others."[8]

The Civil War, dreadful as it was, was also largely a war of principle. At the least, people fought to defend family, home, and their way of life. As far as larger issues went, people shed their blood to oppose slavery and to preserve the Union. Although modern wars tend to be a mixture of principle, economics, and politics, both World War I and World War II were fought to oppose the forces of those who would have enslaved others. World War II, especially, was fought as a war to oppose the erection of a Satanic kingdom, a Beast system. It is my strong belief that nazism, a demonic system which was translated into a political reality, had to be opposed by military force. It is also my contention that since Hitler was a type of the coming Antichrist (the closest spiritual type which history has yet produced), the world had no choice but to oppose him by force of arms.

World War II could perhaps be characterized in some ways by two events: the Holocaust and Hiroshima. The former dispelled any illusions that mankind is by nature good (one of the favorite beliefs of secular humanists). The latter revealed the dangers of science and technology (which secular humanists see as the hope for salvation for the human race). People realized that the Bible is quite accurate when it describes unregenerate man as having insanity in his heart. Hiroshima illustrated clearly that man had finally perfected the ability to destroy the entire planet and everyone on it. Near the end of the war, Hitler inaugurated the age of the ballistic missile. After Hiroshima, everyone understood that the world would never be safe again other than through some sort of internationally mandated cooperation. It was in that hope that the United Nations was born. America, which had sacrificed and suffered so much in order to oppose evil, anticipated that it would enjoy a long period of peace, stability, security, and happiness. Instead, it found itself in an age of anxiety, the age of the Cold War. World War II led not to ultimate victory (for there is no such thing in a secular world), but only to the outbreak of the Cold War. By the time we finally won the Cold War, we were already losing the culture war.

"The years which followed the end of the Second World War in 1945 were marked by innocent idealism. The ghastly nightmare was over. 'Reconstructionism' was the universal goal. Six years of deconstruction and devastation belonged to the past; the task was to build a new world of cooperation and peace. But idealism's twin sister is disillusion."[9]

Linda Bowles, who believes that most Americans are convinced that the country is headed toward socialism and hedonism, believes we can put this trend into perspective by looking at the generation of Americans who won World War II. She writes, "True they won the war, but they lost what came next. They stood around with a strange impotence, overwhelmed by it all, as everything they had fought for and stood for got trashed." She says that "we are witnessing the inevitable denouement of the sorry sagas of the 60s. The bitter fruit of these demons *(sic)*, seeds of the 60s is all around us."[10]

She feels that the moral decadence and slide toward socialism which began in the sixties reached its high-water mark with the election of Bill Clinton. Newspaper columnist Samuel Francis pointed out that in some ways the Clinton presidency was a high-water mark in the culture war. He wrote that "in the Clinton era it is those who defend their culture and moral beliefs from calculated assault that are considered dangerous—not those who are doing the assaulting."

Those whom we have come to know as baby boomers were born between 1946 and 1964, with the first generation of baby boomers coming of age in the 1960s. Their crowning glory was the inauguration of the presidents Clinton. Their coming of age precipitated a major disintegration in the fabric of American society. In fact, "It would be hard to find any decade in American history when so many things went so wrong at once."[11]

This generation rejected the morality and the faith of their parents, rejecting godly absolutes and embracing the philosophies of secular heroes like Marx, Freud, and Darwin. American society thus experienced its first major breakdown in the 1960s as the emerging generation proclaimed God to be dead, and turned instead to drugs, the occult, sex, socialism, and rebellion. It was in this generation that the former counterculture grew up and became institutionalized, the basis of a new American culture.

It was the beginning of what Paul Schenck called the false consensus in his book, *The Extermination of Christianity*. It was the beginning of the rise to power and prominence of what we know as the New Left.

> The New Left are those groups who have assimilated the values of the sixties, including the sexual revolution, radical feminism, homosexuality, abortion, and socialistic structures such as public education, the communal control of resources, and a tacit atheism as national dogma. Those who were the radical left-wingers of the sixties are now those who are labeling Christians as right wing.[12]

Joseph Sobran adds that it is hard to find any standard to show that American society is healthier now than it was in 1950. He noted that we were told to let go of our outdated attitudes, but it turned out that our outdated attitudes were the stuff that held our civilization together. Thus,

> America was overwhelmed by counterculture, heathen hordes whose goals involved the use of public education, the courts and the armed authority of the law to erase traditional distinctions between right and wrong, incite class hatred, subvert religion, undermine the traditional family, redistribute wealth, foster anti-American multi-culturalism, promote a one-world philoso-

phy and produce an egalitarian, collectivist society.[13]

The present breakdown in our society was not only predictable. It was inevitable. It is my belief that in a national sense, things do not just "happen." They are a reflection and an expression of things that are going on in the unseen spiritual realm. This concept is difficult (if not impossible) for secular humanists to grasp. They have no eternal perspective. Their attention is fixed on the here and now in the purely physical realm. We live in a society which has been so saturated with the idea of evolution that people accept it without even stopping to consider the implications of what they believe; that society itself is evolving. It is a sort of informal Hegelian–Darwinian idea that opposing ideas bring a resolving synthesis, a resolution where the stronger ideas, ideals, and people eventually win out in an ongoing march toward perfection. Scientists around the world, however, are seeing only a steady depletion and exhaustion in the universe. There is no indication that anything or anyone is evolving toward any sort of perfection. Things in the physical universe and in society itself are breaking down and moving toward chaos, both in nature and in society. The move toward chaos in society is a planned activity. What happened in the 1960s was not accidental. It was, however, spiritual, since there is a spirituality behind what we call politics.

My hope is to maintain an eternal focus in the midst of the "here and now" activities of everyday life. For example, I am interested in politics, and I believe that Christians should be involved in the political process. I believe in political concepts like Constitutional integrity, limited government, personal freedom, states' rights, and so forth. I do not believe that our salvation (either as individuals or as a nation) can ever come from politics. Salvation comes only from the Lord. That greater allegiance dominates what I consider to be lesser allegiances as the sun dominates the moon. I like the moon a lot, and it does a good job supplying reflected light at night, but it is just not the center of the solar system. Christianity, which is the center of my belief system, illuminates my world view.

Breakdown begets breakdown. At each breakdown, a little more personal freedom is lost. "Many Christians naively believe that the worldwide persecution predicted in Scripture will occur overnight, that somehow on one day we are perfectly free to worship the Lord and speak about him as we wish and the next day it will be illegal to be a Christian. That's not how it works."[14]

Once the infrastructure of society is sufficiently weakened (by a process which I call the Satanization of society), the stage is set for sudden, cataclysmic change. This change, which is often precipitated by some dramatic event (economic collapse, internal insurrection, military defeat, etc.), generally leads to the emergence of a strong political leader who seems to have all the answers to the ills of society. This leader then becomes the driving force behind even more wide-ranging societal and cultural change. We in America have sown the wind and are now reaping the whirlwind (Hos. 8:1–8).

It is important for people to realize that our hope for salvation (both individual and corporate) is not in politics. Our salvation will come neither from the Republicans, nor from the Democrats. It will come neither from the Right nor from the Left. Yet, the elections of November 1994 seemed strangely spiritual to me. By that, I mean simply, that I felt as if God was extending our national lease on freedom and liberty. I felt that God was showering His grace upon our nation—perhaps for the last time. It was an invitation to turn away from our national slide into godlessness so that we might turn again to Him. It was an invitation for a national repentance. In the Bible, repentance does not simply mean saying that one is sorry. It is an embracing of truth and a turning away from wrongdoing. It was almost as if God were saying, "If my people who are called by My name, will humble themselves and pray, and seek my face, and turn from their wicked ways, then I will hear from heaven, will forgive their sin, and will heal their land" (2 Chron. 7:14).

4

The Satanization of Society

I believe in a conspiracy theory of history. (I am not necessarily referring to a cabal of mysterious power-brokers, meeting somewhere behind closed doors—although I am sure that does happen. People like this may certainly wield great influence and help shape human history, but they are not really the main issue. They themselves are also being shaped and used.) I also freely admit that many people see conspiracies where there are none. The opposite is also true. Many people fail to see the conspiracies that do exist. This is especially true of the largest and longest conspiracy of all: the Satanic conspiracy. The Satanic conspiracy includes both the deceived and the deceivers, the willing and the unaware. Satan conspires with a myriad of groups which are not necessarily conspiring with each other to establish his own agenda. He thus works almost invisibly to establish an overall societal mindset.

The dictionary defines a conspiracy as "a group planning and acting together secretly for illegal or harmful purposes." The key to understanding the historical process and purpose is to realize that the true essence of history is spiritual. It is also the key to understanding the human condition. The conspiracy theory is at the center of the entire historical process.

All of history is in a sense the outworking of one great historical theme: the rebellion of Satan and his followers against a holy God. Satan conspired against God in the very corridors of heaven. The result of this celestial conspiracy was the expulsion of Satan and his followers from heaven. They were sent into exile, forfeiting their former high station. Once they were banished from heaven, the conspiracy shifted to earth where Satan set up his own rival kingdom, eventually seducing Adam and Eve into rebellion against God. Satan's success in this endeavor guaranteed the direction that history would take until the end of the age. At that moment humanism and demonism became entwined with the human condition. Once sin entered the world, the future of every person who would afterward be born was affected. A spiritual war had been declared in which there would be no neutrals. Every human being would have to take a stand in this ongoing war. The choice would be both an individual one and an eternal one. The battle would rage around the acceptance or the rejection of God's truth. Pontius Pilate asked Jesus, "What is truth?" Pilate rejected the existence of absolute and universal truth, although it stood incarnate before him. Because he was not willing to receive the truth, to believe that truth is absolute, universal, and eternal, Pilate could never experience the fact that truth is also personal. Pilate, who lived as all men do—one heartbeat from eternity—failed his greatest test by rejecting the truth. Our society is following in Pilate's footsteps.

We are living in a spiritual age. Unfortunately, it is not especially a Christian age. The Bible is quite clear that in the end times, the distinguishing feature of the age will be spiritual deception.

Having rejected the truth, we are now living in an age characterized by false things: false values, false teachers, false hope, false prophets, a false gospel, false churches, false brethren, a false spirit, and even a false Jesus. Some of these things will be such effective counterfeits that they will fool many people—including people who should truly have known better. The goal of counterfeit things is to substitute something which is false for something which is true and to have the false accepted as being true. This, of course, is the primary work of the antichrist spirit in society: to oppose truth and to sow error. False things bear false fruit and deception leads to destruction.

The immediate goal of the antichrist spirit is to steal godly truth from our society and to replace it with "Satanic truth." Satanic truth is designer truth. It is designed to appeal to the pride, rebellion, and selfishness of the unregenerate heart. The ultimate goal of the antichrist spirit is to produce conditions in society that are favorable for the appearance of the Antichrist.

I once heard of a linguist who amused and occupied himself by trying to create the ultimate evocative image by forming expressions of two or three words. I am sure that it is probably a wonderful hobby—truly the stuff from which poetry is made. Just as the oceans can go no farther than the shores which confine them, human effort of every sort is confined within certain parameters. God, however, is the ultimate linguist. I believe that God's eternal bestseller, the Bible, is the most powerful and perfect work of literature which has ever been created. It is filled with wonderful and powerful images. I believe that there is no more powerful descriptive expression in the Bible than "The Abomination of Desolation" (or "the Abomination which makes desolate"). It is an expression which describes the culmination of utter evil and destruction in the person and career of the Antichrist, the central figure

of the Great Tribulation period, the darkest time in all
of human history.

In both the Old and New Testaments, the word
abomination has a highly significant meaning. An abomination described something which God found to be
highly offensive, disgusting, and loathsome. It almost
always had close connections with idolatry and immorality. Prophetically, the culmination of idolatry, blasphemy, and immorality is called the Abomination of
Desolation. It is abomination personified. This term
refers specifically to the Antichrist and his false religious system—a system which will dominate the end of
the age.

This whole scenario is carefully recorded and am-
plified in the prophetic Books of Daniel and Revelation. The prophet Daniel, inspired by the Spirit of
God, wrote a short prophetic picture of what things
would be like at the end of the age, just prior to the
total system breakdown which is recorded in the Book
of Revelation. Daniel described our modern world as
a time of great knowledge, affluence, mobility, and
restlessness. Other Bible references specifically state
that it will also be a time of selfishness and deception.
Daniel prophetically described a world in which there
would be an explosion of knowledge. We are now
living in that prophesied world. Information and knowledge have been increasing exponentially. Modern man
has accumulated so much information and knowledge
that he has been forced to create a whole new growth
industry just to store and process them. Earlier in history, a new invention or a new technology might take
centuries, generations, or decades to change the way
people live and think. Now, a new invention or a new
technology can change the way we live and think almost overnight. It does not stop there, however. New
inventions and new technologies become almost immediately obsolete as newer inventions and technologies
spring from them.

When Solomon said that there was nothing new under the sun, he was not referring to technology. I think that he meant that, unaided by God, the human heart remains essentially unchanged across the millennia. Technology surely changes the way that people live, but it does not change who they are. Only God can do that.

The original Tower of Babel was a monument to man's insatiable desire for knowledge. The Tower of Babel had only institutionalized the choice which Adam and Eve made in the Garden of Eden. By choosing what they considered to be a "good thing," Adam and Eve missed out on what God considered the "best thing": knowing Him. The Bible tells us that a knowledge of God is the beginning of both true knowledge and true wisdom.

Ideas matter. They have both immediate and long-term consequences, for one thing leads inevitably to another. Ideas are the lever which moves people to action, changing the way people live and the way people think. Sometimes the change is for the better, sometimes for the worse. Many Americans in affluent America, for example, are now realizing that although Americans have all that money can buy, the quality of American life continues to deteriorate and decline. They realize something has gone wrong.

With this explosion of knowledge, information, and technology has come the age of manipulative advertising. As Andre Agassi says in a commercial, "Image is everything." Sadly, that has become true to a large degree. Materialism reigns, greed is artificially stimulated, and form replaces substance. Instead of asking, "What is worthwhile?," people want to know "What sells?" or "What works?" The resulting superficiality, stupidity, silliness, and sinfulness feeds the atmosphere of deception. It is all compounded by the fact that the world is rapidly becoming primarily a world commu-

nity of consumers, all profoundly affected by materialism.

Information and communication are shrinking the
world. Words, ideas, transactions, and ideals travel
around the world in seconds. History is no longer
studied from books. We watch it as it is being made
(and reinterpreted) on television. People have the time
and the money to travel anywhere in the world. They
move to and fro with tremendous ease, comfort, and
speed.

The world community is truly becoming knit together in ways that once might have previously been
considered simply inconceivable. This interrelatedness
unfortunately also has several major downsides. Disease can now travel around the world as easily as people
can. Any lethal virus (and lethal new viruses are being
discovered all the time) can board an airplane with an
infected passenger anywhere in the world, and can
easily be anywhere else in the world in a matter of
hours. Local epidemics have the potential to become
international epidemics. This is even more significant
since we are now seeing diseases that modern medi-
cine believed extinct (or basically controlled) making
dramatic comebacks. Viruses evidently have a technology of their own, for we are seeing new strains of
viruses emerging—viruses which are increasingly im-
mune to antibiotics. We are seeing the entire world
community moving ever closer to the possibility of
experiencing the type of devastating killer plagues which
are depicted in the Book of Revelation. Viruses often
flourish in hospitals. If this trend continues, it is possible that the last place a sick person will want to be in
the age of the supervirus will be the hospital.

Thus, we are seeing that both error and sickness
can spread easily and quickly around the world. Much
like many strains of modern disease, error and deception can be very difficult to diagnose in the early stages.

They can thus progress rather unnoticed, eventually leading to a terminal condition. With the new super-viruses, the sudden appearance of symptoms may indicate that the disease is already in a terminally virulent phase. The same thing is also true with error and deception. In the body politic, they will lead to an eventual collapse; to a sudden, cataclysmic breakdown.

It seems that the more man learns, the more he earns; the more he possesses, the more restless he becomes. This is a phenomenon which is increasing as we move toward the end of the age. It is as current as today's news and as old as the story of Cain. Cain, driven from the presence of God, went to dwell in the land of Nod. Nod means "restless." In a way, all those who live outside a relationship with God are living in the land of Nod. Some of them resort to a variety of fruitless hedonistic pursuits in an attempt to fill the void in their lives. Others get involved with a false spirituality. Daniel wrote that men would go "back and forth, to and fro" on the earth. This description suggests a never-ending restlessness, a condition somewhat like the endless crashing of the waves against the shore. Satan himself is described as prowling to and fro across the entire earth. Satan, who was originally Lucifer, the covering cherub and light-bearing angel, was cast from the presence of God because of his rebellion. Those who walk in his steps also walk in rebellion and restlessness—in willing or unwilling allegiance to Satan. The culmination of the process of the Satanization of society will be the appearance of the Antichrist.

It is rather easy to find examples of this process of deception and disintegration in our society. By dint of powerful repetition and through the clever and manipulative use of media, things that were once seen as strange or evil are now accepted as normal. The process is picking up speed. I give as examples of my

thesis things like the acceptance of the theory of evolution, the belief in the cult of self-esteem, the emergence of politically correct thinking, radical feminism,
the acceptance of homosexuality as an alternative
lifestyle, belief in all manner of occult things, the tremendous increase in cultic activity, etc. The list continues to grow.

I call this process the Satanization of society because the Satanization of society reflects three primary
character traits of Satan. He is a thief. He is a liar. He
is a destroyer. The Satanization of society has three
parts: to steal or suppress God's truth, to substitute
demonic truth, and to prepare the way for the emergence of the One World Order and the appearance of
the Antichrist. Once truth has been redefined, it will
be easy to establish a climate which will be favorable
for the appearance of the Antichrist—a climate of chaos,
rebellion, lawlessness, selfishness, and unbelief. In the
right environment, any type of bacteria can flourish,
any type of disease can grow. In the right climate of
deception, a virulent form of destruction can be un-
leashed.

In the coming chapters, I will explore some significant and strategic truths which either have been stolen
from our society or are in the process of being stolen.
These are all truths which were at one time recognized
as being the foundational truths of our society. They
have been sacrificed to the politically correct gods of
multiculturalism, relativity, and toleration.

We shall study the sources, the scope, and the fruit
of this current attack upon truth. We shall also attempt
to establish a fruitful action plan.

5

A Historical Perspective

I suppose that everyone has a biased world view to some degree. Our biases are generally the result of how we have been raised or the result of sincere soul-searching and study. The dictionary defines a bias as "an inclination, temperament, or outlook." There is an old saying that instructs us that "as the twig is bent, so the tree will be inclined." The Bible likewise has much to say about having a sure foundation, a foundation which insures stability.

A bias is a bent. (As a point of reference, it tells us in Genesis 8:21 that "man's bent is always toward evil from his earliest youth." God alone can straighten people out.) The danger is that once people are bent in a wrong direction, they might continue in a wrong direction—right into eternity. Once again, it is largely a question of truth. Philosophers are greatly concerned with epistemology. Epistemology is the study of the theory, nature, origins, and limits of the truth. The man in the street is more concerned with applying the truth in daily living than he is with its more philosophical aspects. The greatest battle in our society is being fought over truth. The Bible instructs us that at the end of the age people will prefer falsehood to truth, and that the prevailing mindset in society will be deception. God's truth will be largely rejected.

I personally have two major biases. The first is my Christian world view. (In order to be as clear as possible, I define Christianity as I understand it to be in a later chapter.) My Christian world view is the lens through which I interpret everything—including history (which is my second bias). I do not claim to be a historian. I have, however, both studied it (and still do), and taught it. I think the study of history is fun. It is also beneficial. I am convinced that only those who have a Christian perception will truly understand the larger historical picture. I am also convinced that those who have a solid historical perspective are harder to deceive and to manipulate than those who don't. Their viewpoint on life tends not to be as superficial and fragmented as is often the norm in our historically illiterate society.

Those who have a true appreciation of American history are a rapidly shrinking minority, and things are only going to get worse. The theft of America's historical perspective is an important part of the remaking of the American conscience, the American consciousness, and the American consensus. Newspaper columnist James Sobran came up with the theory that one way Americans of the 1990s could strengthen their understanding and appreciation of the true legacy of American history would be to study American historical documents. By doing that, we modern Americans would be able to dialogue with our founding fathers. Sobran, for example, read a collection of presidential inaugural addresses. His conclusion was that for well over a hundred years, American presidents were firm in the conviction that the power of the federal government had to remain limited. His greatest concern was that modern Americans have grown too lazy and too poorly educated to converse with our own ancestors.

Dr. Paul Vitz did an exhaustive study of American textbooks for the Department of Education. In his study he reviewed sixty of the most popular textbooks in public schools. His conclusion was that Christianity had been almost totally eliminated from these texts. Authentic Christianity has slowly been replaced by a secular humanist emphasis. This process (which Tim LaHaye calls "the deliberate rape of history") has deprived a generation of young Americans of a true understanding of American history. It is not accidental. Three powerful foundations, which have a major financial impact on American education (Carnegie, Rockefeller, and Ford Foundations), have been heavily investing in the teaching of American history since the early 1900s. Their special emphasis was to "reinterpret traditional American heroes" to the American public. "Dr. Cleon Skousen, a careful research scholar, pointed out that his investigations showed no derogatory accounts of our national heroes prior to 1913."[1]

This supports the conclusions of Tim LaHaye, who researched over six hundred books in the Library of Congress. LaHaye states, "If you wish to find the Christian views of our Founding Fathers, you must go back to books written more than fifty years ago."[2]

The government recently funded a two-year, $2.2 million study of the standards for the teaching of United States history in grades 5-12. Gary Nash, the codirector of the project, announced that their goal was to bring about a new revolution in the teaching of American history. They succeeded in their goal, producing a monument to multiculturalism and politically correct thought. It is also a monument which is based on a rejection of the true spirit and substance of American history. Ben Wattenburg calls it an attempt to neutralize American history. It is a total rejection of George Will's belief that "America is the most important thing that has ever happened." Pat Buchanan calls this the "anti-Americanism of history in our schools," a politicizing of history. Buchanan believes that any nation which subsidizes such assaults upon its history is toying with suicide. American history is so full of greatness and glory that it is simply cowardice to tolerate this ongoing slander against our country.

> Memory is what makes us what we are. History is the memory of a nation and that memory is being erased in schools and colleges across the country. Worse, fantasies are being recorded over the facts in that memory. Whoever controls the past controls the future.[3]

History is a rich field of study. (It is also usually unappreciated by the majority of American students since they regard reading as a terrible chore. It requires both effort and concentration.) History is the branch of knowledge which records, explores, and attempts to explain past events. Charles Colson has said that he believes that the great dialectic of history is spiritual. In this he is in agreement with the great historian, Arnold Toynbee, who believed that all history, once you strip the rind off the kernel, is really spiritual.

As I have said, I am what a friend of mine calls a "history buff." I am also a prophecy buff. Prophecy is simply history written before it happens, by God, the Ultimate Historian. I hope to join these two interests together in this book, illustrating where I believe we have been as a nation, where we are now, and where we are headed as Americans.

Sometimes hints to understanding the present and the future are to be found in the past. From antiquity to modern times, history has taught us two powerful lessons. The first lesson is that the liberty and freedom of the citizens diminishes as the power of the state grows and expands. This process is aided by the apathy and ignorance of the populace. The second lesson is that where religious influence wanes, civilization tends to disintegrate. There was a period preceding the reign of Augustus Caesar called the Time of Delirium. It was an age of chaos and instability—an age which caused people to yearn for security and for a leader who could give it to them.

When Augustus Caesar inherited the throne of emperor, he was slowly able to unite and solidify all the power of the state in the office of emperor, thus becoming one of Rome's most powerful emperors. He used this power to bring about an age of peace, stability, and prosperity. Augustus kept the form of republican government and refused to eliminate the Roman senate. He was thus able to rule as a dictator without appearing to be a dictator.

Upon Augustus' death, the new emperor, Tiberius, offered to give up the powers that Augustus had slowly usurped. The senate didn't want them. The senate, just like all the other Roman citizens, had grown used to the idea of the state (in the person of the benevolent emperor) taking care of them. (The attitude of the state as provider is currently widespread in America. We got a good view of this attitude during the 1994 presidential campaign when a young man asked the candidates what he and his generation could expect the government to do for them.) They greatly preferred comfort and security to liberty. Tiberius thus continued the process of usurpation, eventually instituting the Maiestas Law. Under this law, it became criminal to show either criticism or disrespect to the emperor. Freedom of speech disappeared almost unnoticed and unprotested. It is not possible for a nation to be free when freedom of speech ceases to exist. Gerald Ford set the problems of ancient Rome in a modern context when he said that "a government big enough to give you everything you want, is big enough to take from you everything you have."

Since the presidency of Franklin D. Roosevelt, many Americans have learned to see the ever-expanding powers of the state as the Romans saw during the offices of Augustus and Tiberius.

Since F.D.R., two generations of Americans have been educated and bribed to believe that it is the responsibility of the state to take care of them. They are more than willing to ignore the fact that "the larger the government, the greater the ration of coercion in our lives."[4]

More and more, the government feels it has both the right and the duty to impose its will upon the people it was elected to serve, reflecting Lyndon Johnson's liberal Great Society belief that government can reshape society and civilization. Since then, until now, government has fought a thirty-year battle to "improve" our social life through government programs. Their efforts have been largely counterproductive.

We are seeing the Roman experience being repeated in America. America is moving quickly toward its own maiestas law. Under our version of this law, however, it will soon be a criminal offense to speak out against government-endorsed abortion, euthanasia, or homosexuality. Those in power do not hesitate to use the extensive power at their disposal to enforce obedience.

Many in the government have become increasingly arrogant and corrupted by power. Columnist Linda Bowles writes that "many in the government have become arrogant and corrupt, with an imperial view that those who disagree with or resist their mandates are enemies who must be shut up, shut down, and when necessary, bludgeoned into submission." She asks the question, "Who will protect us from our government?"[5]

Every recent opinion poll reveals that there is a steadily growing distrust among Americans toward the government. "A vast majority of the American people now harbor a deep and abiding cynicism toward their political leaders and toward the once-cherished institutions of government."[6]

Henry Adams defined the American dream as the theory that the American people would be able to limit their government. In our age, that thought has become strictly a quaint political theory. It was, however, the key political thought of our founding fathers, who feared the power of an expansive centralized government. Some Americans (the ones with a historical perspective) share that concern. Thomas Sowell has voiced the opinion that "the growing state power is the central danger to human freedom." This belief caused our founding fathers to see our Constitution as the basis of our freedoms. This amazing document was written to define and limit the power of the federal government. "The sources of this constitutionalism were historical precedents, belief in a Higher Law, limited government, and individual liberty."[7]

Our society has seen individual liberty disappear as the first three historical precedents have been forgotten, or rejected. The Constitution for most Americans is now what the Supreme Court says it is. This is an idea espoused by the Court itself. The Constitution is now seen as an "evolving document." It is in no sense absolute, but may be reinterpreted to reflect the thought of the times.

> The original concept of the Supreme Court was predicated on a belief in a higher power. The same was true of the Constitution. The Supreme Court was to apply in particular cases the Constitutional law which was based on a Higher Law. The court long ago rejected that role. In reality, however, the Supreme Court has no reason for being if there is no Higher Law. The State has become the judge and custodian of human values. In brief, we have forgotten, or

are forgetting the origin and sources of our tradition.[8]

We thus "live in a post-Constitutional America. The 'adaptability' of the Constitution guarantees that it no longer means what it used to—or ever will. The 10th Amendment has been functionally nullified that powers not specifically given to the federal government belong to the state governments and to the people."[9]

Our government continues to aggrandize itself, slurping up the rights of the citizens, establishing ever-greater rights for itself, and rejecting the guiding principles of the Constitution. The government, rather than being limited, is actually the fastest growing American industry. With this growing power comes a growing boldness and a growing determination to become even larger and more powerful.

> It used to be that when the ruling class wanted to get away with blatantly unconstitutional conduct, they were clever enough to contrive tortured interpretations of the law to justify it. Now they don't even have to endure that pretense. They just openly admit that what they are doing is unconstitutional and do it anyway.[10]

In America in the 1990s, our own government not only no longer reflects the values of those it claims to represent, it actively works to suppress and destroy those values. Americans tend to have a naive confidence in the permanence and stability of the institution of democracy. Modern history has some dramatic examples of how both democracies and socialistic states can be corrupted and end up as totalitarian states. Americans need to regain their historical perspective before it happens again.

6

Another Historical Perspective

I believe that the historical process is also a spiritual process. If I am correct in my assumption, it also seems clear that both God and Satan are heavily involved in the human drama which we call history. Satan has two deep and abiding interests, both of which bear heavily on the lives of people: theology and politics. Satan's views on these two subjects are simple. He wishes to be worshiped and he wishes to be obeyed. We shall see both of those desires united in the Beast system of Satan at the end of the age, where he will be both worshiped and obeyed throughout the entire earth. It is toward those ends that he has always worked, and it is toward those ends that he works still.

Politics is the science of government. Its essence is the gaining, maintaining, and using of power. It is only common sense to believe that Satan (the ultimate politician) is closely involved with human politics, since it is his ultimate goal to govern and control. Although Satan has worked toward this goal covertly throughout human history, he will soon work visibly. Meanwhile, I think we should realize that Satan has political preferences. I believe, for example, that he hates the republican form of democracy that has existed in America. There are two diabolically good reasons for this. The first reason is that democracies are harder for him to control, especially democracies of the American type which have clearly separated political powers. History teaches us that freedom is hard to achieve and perhaps even harder to maintain. The American republican democracy was unique because it was founded on a covenant relationship with God. Those who came to make a new life in America came for two primary reasons. They came seeking a place where they might practice their faith. They came as missionaries, as men and women who were committed to establishing a society founded upon scriptural principles. Don Feder wrote that "The origins of American government can be traced to the Mayflower compact, signed by almost all the adult males of the company. Their enterprise, they declared, was undertaken 'for the glory of God and the advancement of the Christian faith.' How monocultural!"[1]

The Pilgrims came to America as the heirs to the vision of (the much maligned) Christopher Columbus. Peter Marshall tells an interesting story about Columbus and about the faithful provision of God. In 1315 the Christian missionary Raymond Lulle wanted to go on one last missionary journey. He decided to take the gospel to the Muslims in North Africa. The Muslims stoned him and left him for dead in the public square. He was found, close to death, by two merchants from Genoa. These merchants took him aboard their ship. As he stepped into eternity, Lulle raised himself up and pointed toward the Western ocean. He told them of a land there that needed to hear of the salvation of the Lord and nearly with his last breath said, "Send men there." This story was repeated and retold many times in the family of one of those merchants: Stephano Colombo. Christopher Columbus was raised on that story. "Christian teachers need to know that while it may not have been the only motivation in Columbus' heart, he felt a divine unction from the Holy Spirit to sail, to find a new land."[2]

This righteous ethic provided strength, inspiration, and vision to the American experiment. Unfortunately, America has largely squandered its cultural heritage, opening the door to disaster. Satan has worked steadily toward that end, for without stealing an appreciation of the true strength and uniqueness of the American heritage, he would be unable to move American society toward the chaos which he requires in order to create a New World Order. America must be overthrown. The first step in Satan's program is to overthrow America spiritually and morally. The second step is to overthrow her politically. Although it has always been admittedly imperfect, the American experiment has been the crowning glory of human freedom in world history. When the flame of liberty is finally extinguished in America, the rest of the world will be dramatically affected.

The second reason that Satan has hated American republican democracy is that religious freedom is truly only possible in nations which love liberty. We are, of course, witnessing an all-out assault in America upon the very thing that has made our nation unique and great: biblical Christianity. Recently, some Jewish organizations have begun to contribute to the attempt to curtail authentic Christianity—seeing it as a threat to Judaism. True Christians, however, cannot be anti-Semitic. To illustrate my point, I quote Michael von Faulhaber, cardinal archbishop of Munich in 1933, who said to the Jews, "I would not understand my own religion, did I not honor yours."[3]

True Christians honor God's calling of the Jews and share a joyful anticipation of their redemption as a nation during the period the Bible calls the Great

Tribulation. True Christians have faithfully supported
Israel since 1948. True Christians want to be both an
encouragement to Israel and a protection to her. Satan, however, hates both Jews and Christians with an
unholy and timeless hatred. Satan opposes the Judeo-
Christian ethic with every means at his disposal. Christianity has become the only minority in our society
which can still be attacked and slandered with impunity. Throughout history there has been a persistent
hostility toward deeply committed Christians on the
part of those wielding power. It is manifest today as it
was throughout history. It will continue to increase
and accelerate as this age draws to a close. As much as
Satan hates biblical Christianity, he loves false religions
of all sorts, working religiously to promote and popu-
larize them. Satan has a vested interest in every false
religion, in every religion which guides people away
from God's truth.

Politically, Satan's preference is the totalitarian state.
His reasons are pragmatic and practical. Totalitarian
states are usually controlled by one strong figure. This
has been the case in modern dictatorships like those in
Nazi Germany, in the Soviet Union, and in China. By
controlling one strong and central figure like Hitler, or
Stalin, or Mao, Satan also controls the whole state. The
definitive pattern for this strategy is explained and
illustrated in the Book of Revelation. Bible prophecy
tells us that Satan will eventually largely control the
entire world for a seven-year period by possessing a
willing human world leader. The Bible identifies this
leader as the Antichrist.

Looking at history with a spiritual eye, we see this
strategy in a lesser form in Nazi Germany, the Soviet
Union, and China. All three leaders and all three re-
gimes bear a strong Satanic imprint. They also shared
some defining Satanic characteristics. All three leaders
are now infamous for their bloodthirsty, wantonly mur-

derous reigns and for their desire for total power and control. They also had in common that they instituted a cultural revolution. They obliterated the existing cultures in their countries in order to establish a new culture more to their personal liking. All three dictators were savagely anti-intellectual and antireligious. All three instituted "cultural revolutions" which were accompanied by ferocious religious persecution, specifically targeting Jews and Christians. Hitler, Stalin, and Mao were profoundly evil by any standard, but the explanation cannot stop there. There was something "other" about them. Their careers give a glimpse into the very mechanics of evil itself. It is my personal belief that they were all previews of the coming Beast kingdom.

It is also my opinion that among the three giants of evil, Hitler stands somehow alone. I believe that Hitler is the closest and most specific type that history has yet produced of the coming Antichrist. By focusing on Hitler as a sort of prophetic lens, by looking closely at his character, methods, and motives, we find ourselves considering what the Book of Revelation calls "the deep things of Satan." It is above all important for Americans to remember and realize that Hitler used the democratic process in Germany to overthrow democracy. Goethe said that coming events cast their shadow before them. Hitler's shadow extends across the twentieth century, for his Satanic task remains yet unfulfilled. By looking closely at the past, however, current and future events will come more clearly into focus. A look at the Third Reich is especially significant in light of the escalating culture war in America. "The Third Reich is a demonstration of the ability of a culture to quickly turn viciously, furiously, even 'uncharacteristically' on what is best within it."[4]

History teaches us that it can happen anywhere. Germany, for example, was a land with a rich Christian heritage—the land of Luther and the Reformation. The Germans, however, sold their Christian heritage for a mass of spiritual pottage. In the 1830s, the German seminaries began to debunk the Bible, subjecting it to what they called "higher criticism." (American schools, which are functionally atheistic rather than neutral as they claim, are now exalting what they call "higher order thinking skills." Both represent the lifting up of man and the rejection of the authority and validity of God's truth.) The German seminaries produced several generations of Christian humanists who held to a form of godliness but who rejected its true power. The German church went to sleep morally and spiritually, forfeiting its role as the conscience of the nation.

Since nothing remains a vacuum, other forces always arise to fill the void. In Germany's case, Teutonic myth, occultism, romanticism, and nationalism began to introduce new spiritual realities into German life. Writers like Nietzsche (who called himself a "pagan to the core," who decreed God dead, and who wrote of exterminating the unworthy) established the cult of the Superman and the exaltation of the self among German youth. Darwin and his evolutionary theories were enthusiastically embraced, as was Hegel's idea of submission to an authoritarian Super-state. They were tied together by the nationalistic, anti-Semitic mysticism of Wagner. Eastern mysticism and Western gnostic thought were united in the occult teachings of the Russian mystic, Madame Blavatsky, who introduced a type of New Age belief system called Theosophy into German society.

Christianity, buffeted and belabored on every side, saw itself becoming more and more politically incorrect, often being labelled as "un-German." The true church, already intimidated and fragmented, grew even more confused as the Laodicean German theologians twisted Scripture to demonstrate that biblical Christianity and nazism were not only compatible, but that their synthesis produced a true form of Aryan Christianity—a hybrid that Hitler called "positive Christianity." Slowly, the Bible and the cross vanished in the churches and were replaced by Mein Kampf and the swastika. The prophet Jeremiah taught that the nations which reject and despise the Word of God will be judged. Germany had placed herself under God's judgment.

The rejection in the 1830s of God's Word bore bitter fruit in the 1930s. Deception is cumulative. Once the fabric of society had been sufficiently weakened, all that was needed was the proper strategic pressure applied to the societal structure to cause it to crumble. Germany suffered two such hammer blows: World War I and the Great Depression. Germany had lost its inner resources and cultural strength and was not able to stand when the flood came. Collapse was inevitable. It was also inevitable that the prevailing climate of discouragement and chaos would prepare the way for the emergence of a strong leader who claimed to have all the answers to Germany's problems. This scenario will soon be repeated.

Germany thought that it was going through a sort of spiritual awakening after having come through an age of disillusionment and cataclysmic change. The Bible warns that disaster is inevitable when people reject the light, and when the light that they follow is actually darkness. Seeking only prosperity, comfort, and security, Germany failed to see the evil which lay behind Hitler. Eventually they lost the ability and the will to resist evil. The rest is history; history which will be repeated.

7

Jews and Christians

American Christians have a lot to learn in the 1990s from the experience of the Jews in Germany in the 1930s. Persecution of the Jews became official state policy when Hitler came to power in 1933. The Nazi state was dedicated to the principles of occult Aryanism and virulent anti-Semitism. The persecution of the Jews in Nazi Germany was therefore not a historical aberration, but a carefully planned and executed event, whose logical conclusion was the Holocaust. To properly understand the depths of evil represented in Hitlerian nazism, and to even begin to comprehend the significance of the Holocaust, it is important to realize that both were planned in the conference rooms of hell before they were executed on earth by those who had given themselves over to the service of darkness and hate.

Hitler clearly announced his plans to deal with the "Jewish question" in his autobiography, *Mein Kampf*. People took his words for sheer bombast and hyperbole. Rational minds were unable to see that those who are possessed by evil are not governed by the principle of rationality, for evil is irrational. But how could Hitler have so seduced an entire nation? How could he have motivated otherwise good people to either accept or participate in the persecution of the Jews, in the attempted extermination of the Jews? It is an important lesson for us to learn, for Bible prophecy tells us that what was a microcosm in Germany will eventually become a macrocosm under the Antichrist. History appears to repeat itself because it does repeat itself. History is a continuum, the outworking of the struggle of good versus evil.

Hitler arose to establish a New World Order by military means. It would be an order based upon spiritual principles—the foremost of which would be the extermination of God's Old Covenant and New Covenant people in order to establish a political religious kingdom which would be ruled by Hitler from a new Babylon. Hitler's hatred for the Jews was motivated by Satan's hatred of the Jews and of God. In Revelation 12, this hatred is illustrated as a type of unreasoning hatred, a demonic and murderous rage directed against the Jews. Satan is the father of lies. He is also a student of Bible prophecy. That revelation enables us to understand the true world view, rationale, and motivation of Adolf Hitler. In Hitler's Aryan occult world view, there was room for only one chosen people—the Jews or the Aryans. Hitler saw the Jews as a threat to the dominance of the Aryan Kultur, and thus, to his own role as the Great Leader. Hitler felt that it was his duty to destroy the Jews in order for the Aryans to continue on their path of world domination and spiritual development. Jean-Francois Steiner wrote that "when people talk about the war of 1939-1945, they confuse two wars which have nothing in common: the one Germany made on the world and a universal war, the war of the Nazis on the Jews, the war of the principle of death against the principle of life."[1]

Many people (me included) feel that these two wars

are actually indivisible. The latter made the former possible. In Hitler's scheme of things, every single Jew had to perish. I believe that Hitler was a willing tool used by Satan in an attempt to break the Word of God. Satan was well aware of God's promise to the Jews to restore them again to the land of Israel. He is also well aware that God's Word tells us that the Jews will yet receive Christ Jesus as their Messiah. In order to nullify those promises, every single Jew had to die. Hitler saw that as his mission. That plan has not changed.

Hitler's methodology in this quest is worth noting. It was refined and perfected as the war progressed. Between 1933 and 1938, 150,000 Jews fled Germany. They escaped because Hitler's political power was not yet supreme and his death machine was not yet fully in place. "It was necessary to invent a killing machine. It had to be inconspicuous and efficient. It had to reduce handling to a minimum."[2]

The murder of so many people caused certain logistical problems—especially in wartime. Hitler's system of control and surveillance, his intense and ongoing propaganda program, and German technology solved most of the problems. The perfection of poison gas within the concentration camp system broke the logjam of victims awaiting execution. Peter Wyden reported that the Germans were inspired to accomplish the task at hand because they were possessed by a spirit of *ordnung* (order). Everything had to be in its slot. Everything had to be neat and tidy, even death.

> One fact played into the hands of the Technicians: the monstrousness of the truth. The extermination of a whole people was so unimaginable that the human mind could not accept it. Everyone knows the famous Nazi principle that holds that the more incredible a lie is, the more readily it will be believed. Inversely, the more incredible a truth is, the less it will be believed.

Such is the human mind which prefers lies to the truth.[3]

"The first step in the progression toward the persecution of persons is identification. The second is marginalization; the third, vilification; the fourth criminalization; and, finally, persecution."[4]

The truly diabolical nature of the Nazi machine enabled it to create accomplices. Those it touched were drawn into its philosophy and practice of evil. Obedience to the state (personified by Hitler) was a principle which had to be unquestioningly respected. In that obedience, the German people accepted the principle of Hitler's leadership and of his new morality. Ruth Andreas-Friedrich wrote that if the Nazi overlords ordered the people "to kill all the chimney-sweeps in Germany with flails, they would go to it and not leave one alive. They would be without passion and without mercy . . . not because they hated chimney sweeps, but because they loved obedience."[5]

Nazism dehumanized both its victims and its servants. Germany, which had once been one of the crowning jewels of Western civilization, had placed itself outside the flow of Western civilization, becoming antihistorical. By following the Pied Piper of death, Germany became a society which gave itself to the rule of death and destruction. "As a general rule, the mass murders were preceded by a carefully orchestrated sequence of violations of rights. Laws defined who was a Jew, and those who were, were compelled to show identification."[6]

The Jews were registered, issued identity cards, and were forced to purchase and wear the Star of David. Many German Jews had become assimilated in the German population and no longer considered themselves to be Jewish. In Germany, however, Hitler decided who was a Jew. "Nazism made many assimilated Jews once again aware of their Jewishness."[7]

The Jews found themselves increasingly isolated within the German population. They also found themselves increasingly targeted for abuse by the German propaganda machine of hate. They were driven out of the mainstream of Jewish society and stripped of all civil rights. Jews were first forbidden to join the Nazi party. They were forbidden to marry non-Jews. The Jews were redefined by the German legal system on an ongoing basis. Jews were forbidden to call themselves Germans. When some Germans began to protest the treatment of the Jews, Hitler simply redefined them as "non-human." Crimes against Jews were no longer crimes. "Jews first lost their property, education, and jobs. The beginning of the end came when they were removed to the ghettoes."[8]

They were first generally confined to their homes, deprived of all information, support, resources, and hope. They were then killed, resettled in ghettoes, or moved to the death camps.

Nazi Germany gave the world a dramatic lesson in the potential for a technological state to use science to enslave an entire population. Nazi Germany was a harbinger of things to come. It was the world's first technological dictatorship. Hitler's surveillance system was the basis of his control of the nation.

Technology has greatly improved man's capability to spy on his neighbor. It has also greatly improved the government's ability to spy on everybody. Technology has given the government an ability to supervise and to regulate the lives of the citizenry a hundred times over and above anything that was available in Nazi Germany. The best (the worst) is yet to come.

President Clinton recently suggested a national data base for the registration of all American citizens. Of course, politicians always pretend to come up with such suggestions for the good of the people, for example, to insure lots of nice social services. From Franklin D.

Roosevelt's New Deal days until now, Americans have grown more and more used to the idea of the government taking care of them. Many Americans feel that is the true reason for government to exist—a notion which is not only antibiblical, but also the opposite of the belief that was held by our founding fathers, who believed strongly in self-reliance and feared government control over the people. A national data base would be a handy tool for those in power to track, monitor, and control the populace. A national data base would lead to a world data base, guaranteeing that those in power could monitor the lives of virtually everyone around the world.

Tied into the proposed cashless society concept, nobody on the planet could buy or sell without government knowledge, supervision, and permission. That idea is, of course, one of the most salient features of the coming Beast empire—the inability of the citizens to buy or to sell without government permission.

A computer chip registration card would only be the beginning. An implanted computer chip would be even more efficient. It would be an easy, painless, one-time procedure. It would also be relatively easy to implant such a chip in the majority of Americans in a short time. If I am correct in my belief, such a procedure would not take place until after the Rapture of the Church. We could thus automatically subtract the total number of missing Christians from the population at large. (The lack of Christian protestation will make it easier for those in power to sell the idea to the populace.) It would be easy to inject each newborn with a computer chip ostensibly for protection. All of those in the armed services would quickly and easily submit to such a procedure when ordered to do so. All those in the social security system (no chip, no check), those who apply for a driver's license, those who receive any sort of medical treatment, and so forth would be easy prey. The possibilities are nearly limitless. The final and full end result of this process could well be the implementation upon earth of the mark of the Beast, the infamous 666. As I stated earlier, it is my personal belief that the Church will be raptured before that event. I realize many sincere Christians disagree with me on the chronology of it all. If I am wrong, I will apologize to my dissenting brethren in heaven. (Of course by then it won't matter.)

If I am incorrect about the timing of the Rapture of the Church, the Church will have to go through some or all of the terrible period which the Bible identifies as the Great Tribulation. If the Church is not removed from the earth before the final and full emergence of the Antichrist (Rev. 6:1), the Church will face the full force of Satanic fury. They will also suffer the fate of the Jews in Nazi Germany. If I am correct in my assumption that the Christians will be removed from the earth prior to the beginning of the Great Tribulation (the second three-and-one-half year period during the period when the Antichrist reigns on earth), the Church will face just the beginnings of tribulation; just the beginnings of what the Jews faced in Nazi Germany.

It is already true that Christians in America are becoming a marked class of people. Christians in America have gone through the process of identification. They are in the process of marginalization and vilification and are headed for the inevitable step of criminalization. The primary agencies in this process are the same agencies which Paul Schenck calls the establishers of the new American culture: the entertainment/news establishment, academia, and the law.

> The irreligious elite, having assumed the helm
> of culture-making in America, have used the
> enormously powerful venue of motion pictures,
> television, news reporting and commentary, the

classroom, and the courtroom to impose their false consensus—drawn largely from the hedonistic notions of libertinism so popular among the radical left-wing of the sixties upon the general public.[9]

The news and entertainment media constantly hammer at the Christian and his lifestyle as foreign to the new, emerging American culture. Christians are constantly painted as intolerant, bigoted, and reactionary (opposed to what the secular humanist elitists call "progress"). Chairman Mao, one of our century's most callous and bloodthirsty dictators, got a lot of use out of the word "reactionary." Chinese reactionaries who were opposed to Mao's particular brand of progress were "reeducated." Many of them were reeducated to death. At present in America, wherever the elitist group holds power, faith (and the actions which spring from faith) lacks any credibility. Faith is almost automatically considered to be simple bigotry and intolerance. Christian-bashing is now the only officially sanctioned and protected type of discrimination. "It is not just Scripture or theology that is taboo. The moral precepts derived in part from Scripture and from western traditions are also out."[10]

Our language itself is under assault by the force of political correctness. Words have been assigned new values (both positive and negative) and new meanings. Russell Kirk called it an assault on things permanent. The word *tolerance* has been redefined. True tolerance originated in a religious context. True tolerance includes open debate. The false tolerance of the 1990s reflects the growing belief that there are no such things as absolutes. Since there are no absolutes, people are free to redefine concepts like morality and normalcy. The "old tolerance" was free to oppose sin, based upon the guidance of godly absolutes. The 1990s version of toleration rejects any ultimate authority, any authority greater than autonomous man. Modern toleration means the right to sin without any recriminations. Modern toleration cries, "Do not dare to judge or criticize my beliefs or my behavior." That is the place where the Church parts company forever with the secular humanist elite in the culture war. That is also the grounds upon which those forces seek to attack the Church. It is likewise upon those grounds that the Church must resist.

The Christian church in Germany had largely lost its witness in German society by accommodating itself to modern theory and to the changing societal conditions in Germany. By choosing to adapt God's Word to the situation in Germany rather than judging what was happening in Germany through the lens of God's Word, the German church opened itself up to deception, and eventually destruction. The German church was unprepared and ill-equipped to deal with the magnitude of evil which descended upon its land through Adolf Hitler and nazism. At the same time, many German Christians did rise to the challenge and ministered to their countrymen and to the Jews at the risk, and sometimes at the cost, of their lives. While the institutional church in Germany largely failed to meet the demonic invasion of their country, it is also true that of all the institutions, groups, and organizations in Germany which could have (and should have) recognized the threat of nazism for what it was and stood up to it, the church alone was at least partially successful. It did not totally lose its candlestick and many German Christians paid the ultimate price, winning the martyr's crown.

John the beloved disciple was given an open door to heaven. He recorded what he saw for our edification and encouragement in the Book of Revelation. Summoned to the very throne of God, John saw the very heart of heaven. Before the throne he saw a sea

of glass, clear as crystal. I believe this sea represents
the eternal ministry of God's Word. It is upon that
Word that we are to take our stand. God's Word is to
be as absolute in our lives on earth as it is before the
throne of God. It is squarely and firmly upon God's
Word that the German church should have taken its
stand. It is upon God's Word, upon the truth, that the
church in America must take its stand. There will, of
course, be a price to pay for that stand. "Everyone who
wants to live a godly life in Christ Jesus will be persecuted" (2 Tim. 3:12). Why? Jesus warned us that "if
they persecuted me, they will persecute you also" (John
15:20). Yet this is not a cause for fear.

In his book, *The Struggle for Men's Hearts and Minds*,
Charles Colson listed some steps for the Church to
follow in the present culture war. He advises the Church
"to discern the false values of this world and to reject
them. . . . We must point people to the Holy Bible in
their search for truth and answers. We must encourage
disciplined Christian living. We must get off the defen-
sive."[11]

We must also remember that the weapons of our
warfare are spiritual.

The politically correct ideas of diversity and
(pseudo) toleration exist primarily as a rejection of
God's absolute truth. This is not new. Mankind has
always sought to be free of God's authority. The Old
Testament comments on this by saying simply that
"everyone did what was right in his own eyes." The
secular humanist elite would read that and say, "Bravo!"
God, who always has the last word, sees it differently.
From His point of view, such behavior calls for judgment. That is largely what the Book of Revelation is all
about.

By definition, truth must be based upon an absolute. Absolute truth is what Francis Schaeffer called
"true truth." True truth cannot be only somewhat or

only sometimes true. In order to be truth, it must be absolute, universal, and eternal. Only then is truth worth dying for. Christians understand the concept of true truth quite well. They also understand that it is the truth of Christ Jesus that sets people free. People can believe this truth or they can refuse to believe it. It doesn't change anything, however, because eventually everybody will be judged by God's truth. His truth does not depend on external validation—neither on opinion polls nor on our Supreme Court. Heaven has already made up its mind on truth, and there is in heaven a truly Supreme Court—a Court whose judgments are perfect.

Most older Americans were brought up to believe that under our American form of democracy we are permitted to believe what we wish. We have likewise believed that we have freedom of speech—that we might publicly speak what we believe. In theory at least.

> In a free and open society, we are all guaranteed the right to think what we wish, say what we will. That freedom (which is a fruit of the heritage of Western civilization) is based on the idea that truth will ultimately win out, if truth is given a fair chance. That's why we don't have to label, demean, or villainize those who oppose our viewpoints. We can simply state our convictions and agree to disagree. Only in tyrannical societies are proponents of the truth feared and shouted down.[12]

In the world of the politically correct, however, freedom must be put through the strainer of relativism, diversity, and toleration. Their job is to be sure that not enough truth gets through the strainer to "adversely affect" anybody. (The removal of the Ten Commandments from a Kentucky school is just such a straining. The rationale was that by having it there, any student fortunate enough to be able to read, might actually do so, and be, well, adversely affected by such a blatant display of truth.)

Those who fail the politically correct litmus test are likely to be labelled insensitive or intolerant (if they are lucky). If they are not quite so fortunate, they will likely be labelled bigots or hate-mongers. "If your goal were to silence your opposition, discredit their character, and dehumanize their image, could it be done with just one word? I believe the answer is yes. Simply accuse them of spreading hate."[13]

Daily, the Church falls more and more into the category of those who practice hate crimes by speaking out against sin. This likelihood turns more and more into a certainty every day, for the specialty of the politically correct Gestapo is the ad hominem attack—an attack directed on a personal level, ignoring both facts and the time-honored tradition among civilized people of honest debate. In grade school, our teachers called it "name-calling." Name-calling is generally based on emotion rather than on logic or reason. In the new arena of ideas, only the politically correct are permitted to indulge in name-calling. This is a blatant attempt at intimidation. It is an attempt to punish expressions of true biblical faith and to eliminate the Christian testimony from the public forum. It is a supreme irony that those who have the answers to the problems of society are those who are the least permitted to give them.

8

What Is a Christian?

Christians have slowly become a politically endangered species in our current politically correct (and spiritually incorrect) age. Like the spotted owl, Christians have also been targeted to become a politically extinct species. I made it clear that I wrote this book from a Christian perspective. It seems, therefore, worthwhile to define the word *Christian*.

What is a Christian? I sometimes think that the answer to this question is currently one of the best kept secrets in America. There was a recent survey taken among a group of people who identified themselves as Christians. They were asked how they knew they were Christians, upon what authority they could proclaim themselves to be Christians. An amazingly high percentage of those interviewed answered that they were Christians simply because they felt themselves to be Christians. I recently read a letter to the editor in a local newspaper. A woman wrote a letter complaining about born-again Christians (as opposed to cultural Christians). In her letter she said, "You don't have to believe in Christ to be a Christian." What she really meant was that one need not be a Christian (a disciple of Christ) to believe in the Christian moral ethic.

A person is not, however, a Christian because he or she was raised in a Christian home. One isn't a Christian because he or she believes specific doctrines, or because one does "Christian things." Instead, a person believes certain things which are translated into actions because he or she is a Christian. What one is, dictates what one does.

The only true explanation of what a Christian is (and how you can become one) is found in the Bible. The Bible is a closed system, explaining and defining itself without recourse to any outside agency or authority. Authentic Christianity is therefore biblical Christianity. Authentic means "true to its definition," and it is the Bible which gives us that definition.

I also recently read a letter to the editor concerning school choice in a Christian newspaper. The writer was opposed to school choice because to him, the public schools provide a "crucial, culturally uniting influence" which is currently sorely needed in our nation. He saw public education as "providing a shared common experience," as a safety valve which can help deter the current polarizing among groups in our society, which is leading us toward anarchy and perhaps civil war. That is one of the great things about a democracy. Everybody is permitted to have an opinion and given the freedom to express it. I certainly agree with the writer that our country is fragmenting. I also agree that it is polarizing. I just disagree with his proposed solution. Public schools are partially responsible for the fragmentation in society. They are also largely on the wrong side in the culture war.

I see societal fragmentation as being a prophetically indicated signpost for the end times. David Aikman (author of the novel, *When the Almond Tree Blossoms*) believes that we are indeed headed toward a civil war. He sees it, however, as a civil war which will be fought around the concept of values, not around issues like race. He sees it as a struggle between the forces which stand for chaos and those which stand for wholeness and integrity. (In the New Testament, Jesus announced that He came to make men whole. *Integrity* means wholeness in Greek.)

This struggle, of course, has been an ongoing struggle throughout history. Christ has stood for integrity and Satan has stood for anarchy and chaos. Those who stand for Christ work toward soundness and integrity. Those who stand for either Satan or the rule of self are on the side of chaos. Selfishness promotes chaos by divorcing people from the fruitful basis of the main flow of civilization.

Traditionally, morality and conscience have served to protect the human race, opposing all that is fragmentary and temporary. Of course, history has shown us that conscience and morality are not possible outside of a true relationship with God. Simple religion will not do the job. Holy wars, crusades, and inquisitions have proved that. Modern man, however, prides himself on the fact that he has outgrown God.

This growth spurt, however, has only led him to more religion. It has led him full circle to the religion of secular humanism, a religion where man can worship what he has always loved most—himself. Unfortunately, secular humanism is currently America's largest religion. (Our Supreme Court ruled secular humanism to be a nontheistic religion in 1961 and 1964.) Secular humanism is not a tolerant religion, especially where Christianity is concerned. What it cannot suppress, it seeks to incorporate and redefine. The celebration of Christmas for example, was originally a celebration of Christ. If you watch the multitude of ever-proliferating talk shows, you see one major theme now being celebrated when it comes to Christmas. That theme is a pseudo-spirituality, a celebration of the god within, or a celebration of feelings. That celebration is, of course, nothing more than the celebration of man, the true essence of secular humanism. S.I. Hayakawa once said that "cow one is not cow two." Spirituality one is also not spirituality two.

Prior to both World War I and World War II, Germany felt that it was undergoing a great spiritual revival. As a matter of fact, it was. Unfortunately, their spiritual revival was not Christian. It was a Luciferian false light that they perceived and followed down the road to destruction. Such false pied piper experiences always diminish God as He truly is and exalt some false deity (including secular humanism and other false religions) in His place.

Barbara Reynolds wrote a Christmas opinion piece for *U.S.A. Today*. She felt that Christmas gives people the chance to imitate Christ. All human beings are capable of good works. I suppose this is because they have been created in God's image. Any imitation of Christ will assuredly be a blessing to people. Unfortunately, however, no true imitation of Christ is possible. Both Christ's motivation and His empowerment were of divine inspiration. The true source of Christ's actions (even including sacrificial death) was not man-centered, but God-centered. Jesus did what He did in righteous obedience to the Father, to please Him and glorify Him. Righteousness is a right relationship with God. Righteous actions flow from that source.

Ms. Reynolds cites guru Marianne Williamson who perceives "a new spiritual revolution, a new spiritual mood, a new spiritual Renaissance sweeping the world." I agree. Sadly, however, much of what seems to be a spiritual renaissance is the stuff from which the German spiritual renaissance came. Ms. Reynolds ends by saying that "Christmas is not just about sacred history, but a chance for a divine future based on a new spiritual order." Christmas "is," however, about sacred history—about the specific time when heaven invaded earth, and when God the Father freely offered salvation to the world in His Son. That is the true basis of the historical process. Jesus Christ is the Alpha and the Omega, the source and the goal. Apart from that revelation, there will be no divine future. Christmas is not a celebration of a Christ-spirit or of any divine spark within. It is a celebration of Jesus Christ—a celebration of who He is, what He did, what He is doing, and what He shall yet do!

Very few people (no matter how unartistic) would probably mistake a block of marble or granite for a statue. (I say probably because we live in a time and a place where the cultural elite pretends that urine in a jar and pictures of corpses are art.) Michelangelo is the greatest sculptor ever to have lived. Michelangelo had a unique perspective on sculpting. He felt that his job was to use his God-given talent to liberate the human form that was trapped within the marble. The block of marble and the finished statue were of the same essence. The difference was the vision, skill, and labor of the sculptor. As far as Christians go, we are the marble, God is the sculptor. It might be easier to illustrate what a Christian is by first explaining what he or she isn't.

The first thing a Christian isn't is self-made. Just as it is clear that no statue sculpts itself, nobody can make himself a Christian—not by study, not by good intentions, not by effort, not by good works. The most famous line of poetry ever written by Joyce Kilmer is the simple statement that "only God can make a tree." Only God, the ultimate botanist, the ultimate sculptor, and the ultimate everything else can make a Christian. He is the potter. We are the clay.

Nobody is born a Christian. Every human being (despite what psychology preaches) is born separated at birth from God by Original Sin. God, who is love, has made a way for people to come back into a relationship with Him, by establishing a sure and solid bridge across the chasm of separation. This initiative came from God, not from man. All of man's best religious efforts (good intentions, good deeds, fasting, meditation, etc.) are of no avail. The born-again experience is the bridge that God has established across the chasm of separation. It is in the born-again experience that the Holy Spirit causes man's spirit to come alive to God. The Spirit of God brings light, life, and love into a human heart. It is the Spirit of God that places people into God's Church, the body of Christ. People can join churches, but the Holy Spirit alone can add to the Church universal.

The Bible calls Christians "a peculiar people." This does not mean that they are strange (except to the world). It means that they are unique and extraordinary; God's special treasure (Exod. 19:5). They are unique because they have been chosen personally by God and have personally responded in love and faith to His message of redemption (1 Cor. 1:1-2).

Christians were first called by the name *Christian* at the city of Antioch. It is a name packed with power and responsibility. Before that, they were simply called believers. They knew in whom they believed (1 Pet. 1:21). They also knew personally the One in whom they believed. Christianity suggests a relationship and an identification with Christ. They were also called those "of the way." Christians know that Jesus is the only way to God, the only truth, and the only life. Christianity is not a set of beliefs. It is a relationship. It is primarily what one *is*. It is only secondarily what one *does*. Christianity is internal first, then external.

Christians are named for Jesus (Eph. 3:15). They bear His family name because they belong to Him. *Jesus* means saviour (Matt. 1:21). It is by our faith in

Jesus Christ alone that we are saved from Satan, sin, death, and hell. Christians have been redeemed or ransomed. They have been purchased with a price: the blood of Jesus. They are not in business for themselves. They belong to Jesus. He is their source and their goal (1 Cor. 6:19-20).

Christ means "the anointed one." He was anointed by the Holy Spirit of God. The Holy Spirit is the Spirit of both God the Father and Jesus the Son. Every Christian that has been born again has the very life of God inside him. They took on themselves the name of Christian when the Holy Spirit joined them together eternally with the Lord Jesus Christ. They identify with Him because they are part of His body. They have His name, His nature, and His viewpoint. Christ is being formed within them by the power of the Holy Spirit (Gal. 4:19). They commune and communicate with God by the Spirit of God. Their greatest pleasure is to do His will.

Christians have been adopted into the very family of God (Gal. 4:5). They are neither strangers (Eph. 2:19) nor simply servants of God. They are of the household of God. They know God (John 17:3) by knowing Jesus and they fellowship with Him. They are legal citizens of the kingdom of God. Their king is their brother, Jesus. They serve Him voluntarily as love-slaves. Yet these slaves of love are also princes and princesses of the kingdom of God. They are co-workers with God (1 Cor. 3:9). They produce works which last and which bring glory to God.

Christians are "Christ bearers." This means that they carry the Lord Jesus Christ into every situation and into every activity of their lives. Where they go, the Lord goes! Where they are, there the kingdom of God has come! They are salt and light, enemies of corruption and darkness. They preserve and dispel darkness by witnessing to Jesus Christ as Lord. Their lives are

Bibles where people can read all about the lordship of Jesus Christ. They are princes and slaves, redeemed children of God, salt, light, living Bibles, Christ bearers, disciples, and vessels.

When God has a vision, he seeks a vessel. When He has a job to be done, He looks for a man. He looks for a man with a yielded heart which He can fill with His own living presence. He chooses people through whom He can manifest His character, and through whom He can accomplish His will.

God does not choose his vessels by means of outward appearance, or by the standards that the world holds so dear. He is not interested in stars, v.i.p.'s, or in self-made people. He chooses instead weak and foolish things in order to confound the wise, looking for good and fertile hearts which He can train. His method is to train those who He has chosen through fellowship with Him. They learn the lessons illustrated by the life of Christ Jesus: humility, obedience, sacrifice, faithfulness, and love. Life itself is the laboratory in which they are trained after having first been set apart to Him personally in order to be trained. There is no sanctification without separation.

The call into discipleship comes from God. We simply respond. God's disciples are called to be learners and teachers. They are carefully and precisely handcrafted in terms of God's vision for their lives. They are crafted as priceless objects *d'art*, created, however, to be useful, not decorative. They are God's workmanship (Eph. 2:10) created for good works. They are chosen and trained to glorify Him, to bear His name, to share His nature (2 Pet. 1:4), to live by principle, to identify with Him, and to accurately represent Him to others. Once they are fully trained, they will be like Him. They are more than servants, however, for they have the right to call Him "Abba, Father." God the Father is their daddy, and they are His family, His beloved children, with all the rights and responsibilities of true children—both now and throughout eternity.

Christianity is discipleship. The word *disciple* means "learner." A person enters voluntarily into a discipleship program. Such a program of discipleship requires great commitment, faithfulness, and perseverance. It is rigorous training designed to eventually produce fruit in the life of the disciple. Jesus carefully chooses His disciples, trains them, equips them, and empowers them to go forth in His name. They are expected to bear His name, to manifest His character, and to implement His plan. That is what it means to be a Christian.

9

Considerations on Culture

In order to focus on our present cultural dilemma, I thought it would be interesting to go back in human history to a time when the human race had the opportunity to have a fresh cultural start: the Tower of Babel. In those days mankind had already achieved what mankind has been seeking to achieve ever since—a unified world; a one-world government. Unfortunately, God judged this effort because it was a unity built around evil and rebellion. The Tower of Babel summarizes and unites two major concepts: arrogance and confusion—or arrogance leading to confusion. Mankind has always had an inexhaustible supply of arrogance. The Tower of Babel was an architectural tribute to man's ego, a proclamation that man does not need God, a defiant declaration of his independence. The Tower of Babel was also the center of the world culture of the time—as well as the seat of all false religion. It was the merging in ancient times of what we now call secular humanism and what we have always called demonism. When God rained on proud mankind's parade at Babel, people were forced to go forth through-out the whole earth, forming cities, establishing societ-ies, and creating individual cultures. Mankind had great new opportunities. Unfortunately, Satan went with them. To leave the presence of God is to move toward the domain of Satan.

George Otis, Jr., has a unique and interesting per-spective on culture. It is unique because it is spiritual. He believes that culture is a door by which God (or Satan) engages a specific nation or people. He believes that the nations which went out from Babel rejected God's invitation and continued to practice types of false religious beliefs. Instead, they chose to either make or extend already established contracts and covenants with Satan. To the extent that these nations gave them-selves to Satan by the practice of false religions, he reigned in varying degrees of power, manifesting in specific cultures all the characteristics and symptoms of deception and destruction which he incarnates. It is thus that he has maintained his hold upon much of mankind as the god of this world.

It is my belief that American society (which was founded in covenant relationship with God) is now seeking to rebuild the Tower of Babel in American culture. God, of course, has faithfully maintained a strong presence and witness in America. Our land has been tremendously blessed by God. We may, however, be approaching the stage where the line between grace and judgment is drawn according to the "ten righteous people" theory in Genesis 19.

The powers of political correctness pretend to believe that all cultures are equal (except for the American culture which they detest). They preach that none is better than the others, none is worse (except ours), at least under the rules of the politically correct ideal of diversity. Pat Buchanan hit the nail on the head when he wrote that "to call all cultures 'equal' is

Political Correctness at the expense of truth."[1] The present culture war is a war for the truth.

God, who is quite literally above it all, has a somewhat different viewpoint. If God's view is correct, the bottom line is this: cultures which facilitate a relationship with God (according to His truth) are—dare I say it—superior. Those which discourage a relationship with God are lacking in God's eyes. They are actually also counterproductive to the true purposes of history. The reason for this is simple. God has always worked to unify people around a central (and eternal) theme: the lordship of Christ. Time-bound secular humanists have always longed for a perfect earthly society—a society of their own making, created in their image rather than in God's. Unfortunately, human perfection can never be attained in a fallen world. Christ alone will one day make all things new. The job of the Church is to seek to conform culture to God's Word rather than conforming God's Word to human culture.

In the meantime, it is important for us to realize what is happening, where we are headed, and what our responsibility is. Culture is a continuum. It is the sum total of all that has nourished it throughout the centuries. It is the basis of what we were, what we are, and what we and our children will be. Culture is made up of many component parts: our customs, history, literature, folklore, religion, philosophy, art, politics, entertainment, etc.; in short, all that we have shared in common as a nation. Culture is based on a commonality. If that commonality is ungodly (or based upon the worship of false gods), disaster is inevitable.

No matter what the secular humanist crowd believes, American culture is the crowning glory of Western civilization. It is a historical fact that the strength of the American culture was its Judeo-Christian heritage. Its genius was that America was able to grow everstronger as a melting pot. Historically, the uniqueness of American society was that our nation was willing to accept as a national treasure the cultural legacies of those who were drawn to our shores from around the world seeking the things embodied in our elegant hostess, the Statue of Liberty. We borrowed from them all. Our true genius, however, was that we served as a melting pot, a place where diverse peoples were bonded together into Americans; sharers and participants in the American culture. We believed our national motto of E Pluribus Unum. Well, until recently. In recent times we have reversed that motto, single-mindedly pursuing not national unity, but national fragmentation, not truth but truths. Such fragmentation leads only to chaos. We are already experiencing major chaos in our society, but the worst (far worse) is yet to come. People may also be surprised to learn that such chaos is a very carefully planned activity. Just as God works to unify around Christ Jesus, Satan works to bring disunity, disharmony, disintegration, and chaos. Chaos is his medium. It is his goal.

The incredible thing about our age is how quickly our nation has turned its back on our cultural heritage. The lesson that history has taught us over the millennia is that no multicultural society has ever succeeded. The most recent examples of this can be clearly seen in the ongoing disintegration of the former Soviet Union and in the terrible bloodbath the world recently witnessed in the dreadful ethnic conflict in the former Yugoslavia.

It is in the corruption of the German culture by Hitler and by nazism that we most clearly see the alarming possibility of a civilized nation committing cultural suicide by turning against its Judeo-Christian heritage. Cancer is a disease in which the body insanely turns on itself. Hitler was a type of cancer in the German body politic. We are seeing the same scenario emerging in America. America is now rejecting the basis of its own culture. Hitler introduced a new paradigm in Germany. "A new paradigm" is one of the favorite expressions of the secular humanist (New Age) elite.

The dictionary defines the word *paradigm* as a "model, example, or pattern." A new age requires new viewpoints, new goals, and new standards. Implied in a new paradigm is the rejection of the old paradigm, specifically, the Judeo-Christian ethic and the entire historical flow and perspective of Western civilization.

Substantial change usually comes rather slowly, in incremental steps. These steps may eventually lead to sudden sweeping changes—rather like the swing of a pendulum. The idea of a new paradigm within the New Age concept is neither a slow change nor a pendulum change. It is a totally new orientation, the basis of a totally new reality; an abrupt and totally new model of reality and normalcy. This is the fate which potentially awaits our nation if we are successfully reeducated and reoriented by the secular humanist elite into accepting the need for a paradigm. (I must reemphasize that the false religion of secular humanism will lead eventually to overt demonism).

The liberal, secular humanist elites have never controlled our nation by strength of numbers. They control the population by controlling strategic areas of society. These are areas through which they can mold the rules to favor them (the government and the courts)—areas through which they can "reeducate" the public (the media and the schools).

Speaking of education (and I will have much more to say about the crucially important topic of education later), our schools (preschool through university) have already begun to fall under the sway of a new paradigm. Western civilization is no longer in vogue. Politicians and pseudotolerant denizens of the politically correct academic crowd chant, "Hey, hey, ho, ho, Western Civ has got to go." They want to rewrite both history and civilization so that their own fragmenting agendas will each get their share of the pie. It doesn't matter a whit if what they are celebrating has no connection to the truth. Western civilization has historically been the banner-carrier for the Judeo-Christian ethic. It has also been the driving force behind most of the best things about the human condition for several thousand years. This heritage is the true basis of the greatness of America, the basis of our understanding of who we are as a nation. If American history is the memory of our nation, our nation seems to have entered into a period of national amnesia. In the new scheme of things, however, Western civilization must go. It must be slain and dismembered so that the circling politically correct cultural vultures can greedily gorge themselves on its remains, all the while squawking "tolerance and diversity!"

The elites in our politically correct society are currently in love with the ideas of toleration and cultural diversity. (Song writers through the ages have often discussed the ability of such infatuation to people who are blind to truth's harsher realities.) The reason for this attachment is simple. They are in rebellion against the demands made upon them by a holy God. These people reject the idea of godly absolutes. To them the greatest virtue is to have the freedom to do exactly as they please. They prize the ability of choosing what they believe to be true. One of the main tenets of the New Age movement is that people make their own realities. What is true for them is what they choose to believe. (Charles Manson is an excellent example of this philosophy.) Truth thereby becomes debased in society, and we return to Old Testament times where "each man did what was right in his own eyes."

People demand the right to privacy—the privacy to believe what they want and to do as they please. There is no such thing as privacy from God. Toleration is the glue that holds this system together. They pretend that nobody has the truth and that all cultures and all people are thus equally viable and worthwhile. Since there is no absolute truth, the greatest virtue in society is simply to endorse the right of all the others to believe what they want—even if it is opposite what you believe. Both are right.

Silly, huh?

Not as silly, however, as the recent advent of the white buffalo. A female white buffalo was recently born on the farm of a man who raises buffaloes. According to ancient native American (they used to be Indians) prophecies, the birth of a white, female buffalo would be the sign that peace would soon come to the world and that the world would finally live in unity. There was a male white buffalo born earlier in this century, but he didn't count (animal genderism?). The new baby buffalo has been drawing pilgrims from around the country and around the world.

I admit it is sort of a cute buffalo, but I am surely not willing to see it as the way to salvation or world peace. The television reporters interviewed an old gentleman who insisted that the white buffalo is the fulfillment of ancient prophecies, a sign from heaven. He said, "The birth of this white buffalo is as important (presumably not for native Americans alone) as the birth of the baby Jesus." (Aw c'mon!) Of course, to doubt such things is to be intolerant, insensitive, and politically incorrect, especially since the New Age movement has given native American religious ceremonies new significance by highlighting them in the media.

Unfortunately Christians cannot be tolerant of either sin or error. We take our stand on God's absolute truth. Christians are not called to be politically correct. They are called to be spiritually correct. God's absolute truth also has the advantage of being timeless, universal and personal. In fact, "true truth" must be absolute before it becomes personal. Our society seems to have that backward.

I have a friend who works as a prison chaplain in the New York state penal system. He recently attended a meeting with other prison chaplains. The guest speaker addressed them on the topic of multiculturalism. I have taught World Cultures and I clearly find it interesting and worthwhile to understand a bit about other cultures. For a Christian, the study of culture is not an end in itself. It is a tool. At any rate, when the speaker had finished his presentation, he asked if there were any questions. My friend raised his hand and asked, "Doesn't Jesus Christ supersede culture? Is He not the only way to true unity?" He said that you could have heard the proverbial pin drop. The speaker then basically said, "Well, thanks for your input. Any more questions?"

The truth is that either Jesus Christ is Lord of all or He isn't Lord at all. If He truly is what He (and the Bible) claims to be, He is ultimately the answer to all the questions which a study of culture might pose. I realize that in the short term that might be a source of disunity. That was true in the days when Jesus walked the earth, and it will continue to be true until the return of the Lord in glory. The answer, however, is not to suppress the truth. The answer is to tell people the truth so that they can come to their own conclusions and make their own decisions. That is the job of missionaries foreign and domestic. In this task, every single Christian is a missionary.

> The basis of missionary appeals is the authority of Jesus Christ, not the needs of the heathen. The aim of the missionary is to do God's will, not to be useful, not to win the heathen; he is useful and he does win the heathen, but that is not his aim. His aim is to do the will of his Lord.[2]

10

The Fragmentation of Culture

Simply stated, God works to unify and Satan works to bring disunity into the lives of people. God unifies only according to His own terms. He unifies around His Son, Christ Jesus. He unifies through truth.

Unity has always provided a certain degree of protection—both for individuals and for societies. By unity, I mean the unity provided by a corporate holding to the truth. In the case of America, the Judeo-Christian consensus has been the primary unifying factor of our society. This ethic was the glue which held the society together and which gave it hope.

When Abraham Lincoln said that "a house divided against itself cannot stand," he was referring to the potential collapse of our nation due to the Civil War. Lincoln took his reference from the Bible (Mark 3:25, Luke 11:17). Satan's efforts to bring disunity (the politically correct word for it is "deconstruction") take many forms. One of his most successful works in tearing the fabric of our nation is the tremendous fragmentation caused by the question of abortion. Abortion is the primary social issue of our times, perhaps the primary cause of division in our society. I will deal with that in a later chapter. In the meantime, we shall look briefly at a variety of other ways across the wide spectrum of society in which Satan is actively seeking to cause America to implode, to make America a house divided.

Ecclesiastes 4:12 tells us that a cord of three strands cannot be easily broken. This is especially important in times of national and individual crisis. The American Revolution was described as the times that tried men's souls. Ben Franklin summed this crisis up when he told his fellow dissenting Americans that they either had to all hang together or most assuredly they would all hang separately. Julius Caesar, one of the ancient world's most able generals wrote of the principle of dividing and conquering—a tactic since used by many dictators.

The world has always yearned for unity. This is the great driving delusion of those involved in the New Age movement (whose bottom line is the One World Government). The world has remained fragmented despite mankind's best efforts to attain unity. The League of Nations failed. The United Nations is failing. The conclusion of those who want to see the unity produced by a world socialist state (all for the greater good of mankind) is that it must be enforced from above by somebody with the resources, power, and will to do so. Of course, the conditions must first be right.

The first step in this process was to destroy traditional values, values which provided strength, protection, and unity. The second step in this process was to introduce new values. Francis Schaeffer believes that the impoverishment of values leads to two shattering consequences. The first is a populace which seeks comfort and privacy above all things. People in this condition are willing to trade more and more personal freedom to insure that they will be able to maintain their idols of comfort and privacy. The second is chaos caused by a self-centered society. Selfishness always fragments.

That chaos will lead to the emergence of a power elite.
This elite

> will offer us arbitrary absolutes, and who will
> stand in its way? Politics has largely become not
> a matter of ideals—increasingly men and women
> are not stirred by the values of liberty and truth—
> but of supplying a constituency with a frosting
> of personal peace and affluence.[1]

The selfishness which leads to chaos and fragmentation is a carefully planned activity. Fragmentation
within society is necessary in order for Satan to take
control. Satan uses people to carry out his plan. It is
his plan to attack and remake all the institutions in
society which have traditionally provided a protective
influence in society. In this chapter we shall be studying a few of the ways Satan is seeking to fragment our
society.

Satan is an excellent politician. He understands
how to gain and use power. He also knows how to use
the politicians who are pursuing power for themselves.
Politically, catastrophes which induce societal chaos are
an excellent means of population control. Population
control means that those in power will stay in power.

These chaos-inducing events may be either real or
fabricated, but the end result is the same. This is the
basis of the mechanism which can be set into motion
under the Federal Emergency Management Agency
(FEMA) provisions—provisions which will lead to a suspension of the Constitution and the establishment of
martial law. Included among such emergency situations are financial collapse (which, of course, could
easily be caused by financial manipulation by those
who hold that power), terrorist activity ("Both in individual nations and in the overall world the widespread
use of political terrorism has become one of the phenomena of the age."[2]), internal insurrection, foreign

invasion, or threat of foreign invasion. An economic breakdown is almost guaranteed. "History indicates that at a certain point of economic breakdown people cease being concerned with individual liberties and are ready to accept regimentation."[3] "When our economy begins to falter, we will certainly lose our liberty and our freedom as surely as if we should lose it in war."[4]

I'm sure that list could easily be expanded to include some sort of ecological disaster, real or imagined. It is important to keep in mind that there is a powerful elite in our nation (which is also active internationally) whose goal is to expand and solidify its control. In her book *Goddess Earth*, Samantha Smith tells of a secret meet-and-discuss group of elite powerbrokers who conspired against their own people in order to find ways to maintain political and economic power. This committee concluded that "war is necessary and even preferable, as a way to stabilize a society."[5] They also realized that after Vietnam, the American people would not tolerate another war. They decided, therefore, since war was not possible at that time, other agendas had to be found and pushed in order for this elite to maintain control. They decided that they had to find "new enemies."

The struggle against these enemies would replace an actual war. (Hitler, of course, came to power in Germany as a man who would fight the enemies of the German people: the Jews, the Bolsheviks, the criminals, the immoral, the defeatists, the inferior.) Our nation has announced wars on poverty, drugs, and crime in recent years. There are wars which cannot be won in the traditional sense, but if Samantha Smith is correct, they serve the purpose of expanding the control of government. She suggests that the ecological agenda also serves this purpose very well in everything from domestic and worldwide population control to the creation of work forces and police forces to "protect the planet."

The founders of the New Age movement believed that for the New World Order to succeed, worldwide chaos is necessary. The bottom line of the New Age movement is the New World Order concept. It is in the New World Order that spiritual and political control will meet (just as they did in Nazi Germany) in the worldwide kingdom of the Beast. The occult poet W. B. Yeats (who anticipated the coming of the Antichrist) wrote these lines in his poem, "The Second Coming:" "Things fall apart; the center cannot hold. Mere anarchy is loosed upon the world."

This chapter (along with most of the other chapters) will make little sense to those who do not accept the existence of a personal devil, a being implacably devoted to the deception, corruption, and destruction of the human race. I can sympathize with those who don't, for once upon a time I was also too enlightened to believe in what I considered to be a superstitious, medieval belief. I now know better. So, one day, will all of those who hold to my former world view.

There will be a time in the near future when Satan will become visible to all. At that time he will demand to be worshiped. At that point, all those who refused to accept the Bible revelation on the validity of the existence of Satan will learn too late about the perfect accuracy of God's Word. In the meantime, it usually serves Satan's purposes better to work invisibly. Satan is a liar, a thief, and a destroyer. How does he work in society? He works according to his nature. He lies, he steals, and he destroys. He often makes himself more palatable by disguising himself as an angel of light. This is his Luciferian disguise. Those who work for Satan (either knowingly or unknowingly) only naturally manifest the same characteristics as their boss. They lie, they steal, and they destroy. This is true in the physical realm of course, but it is even more true in a spiritual sense. Those who work for him also wear a

Luciferian disguise, posing as benefactors of mankind. Some of them, blinded by pride (Satan's original sin), actually believe they are benefactors. Just as the most efficient type of deception is self-deception, the most effective deceivers are those who are themselves deceived.

Jesus told His disciples that His work was to do the will of His Father. Satan's work is to live in defiance of God and to enforce his will upon the human race. His goal is to control mankind totally. He seeks to be obeyed and worshiped. In order to control mankind, he must in a sense bring them down to his level. Although evolutionists believe that mankind is a product of random evolution, the Bible tells us that mankind was created by God in His image. To be created in God's image means that mankind was created to fellowship with God, to know Him, and to have the deepest possible ethical and moral identification with Him. This identification is predicated on an acceptance of His truth. The first step in this process is that man's spirit, which had grown cold and dark toward God because of sin, must be illuminated by hearing and receiving God's truth. Truth is light. It is ministered to our hearts by the Holy Spirit. Light brings life: eternal life. Satan works to deprive people of God's light and God's life. His substitutes (which are, of course, dressed up to look like viable and palatable choices) bring only darkness and death. It is Satan's plan to steal the truth from society so that he might more easily corrupt people, remaking society in his own ethic and moral image.

Ideas do have consequences—both in the life of an individual and in the life of a society (which is only a collection of individuals gathered into a community around key ideas). I believe Satan has a special and specific hatred for America. It has long been an impediment to his plans for world domination. America was founded as a nation in a covenant relationship with God so that it would be a light to the world. The historical consensus of our culture was clearly Christian from the founding of our nation until after World War II. This cultural consensus provided a certain amount of moral and ethical protection for Americans, as well as the basis for our national vision. Satan realized that this consensus had to be attacked and subverted if he hoped to accomplish his plans in America and worldwide. I realize that the politically correct crowd would find my beliefs about America highly offensive on two counts: my strong belief in the beneficial impact that America's Christian heritage has had both domestically and on a worldwide basis and my strong belief that American culture has been superior (although clearly not perfect) in the modern world. But guess what? I'm right.

In that light I was recently delighted to read of the decision made by the school board in Tavares, Florida. They decided (to the horror of the local teacher's union which endorses cultural relativism) that the instruction of their teachers should include a study of the things that would help students appreciate their own culture. (The actual bottom line of the politically correct movement is that every culture is worthy of respect—except ours.) They mandated that students in the schools of Taveres would be exposed to and taught about our unique republican form of government, capitalism, our free-enterprise system, patriotism, strong family values, freedom of religion, and other "basic values that are superior to other foreign and historic cultures." A revolutionary idea like this might lead to even more extreme beliefs. It might cause a political and cultural revolt against the cultural elite agenda.

Truth will usually win out when it is given a free hearing in the public forum. That isn't likely to happen. The secular humanist crowd regards truth like health organizations regard the flu. They must seek to prevent an outbreak at all costs, for they have a lot to lose. Nobody knows where such an infection might lead. If thousands or millions of people came down with an infection of truth, secular humanist-demonic philosophies would share the experience of the witch in the *Wizard of Oz.* All her beautiful wickedness melted away because of one little dose of water! A little truth likewise goes a long way; from here to eternity.

Unfortunately, the Taveras story did not have a happy ending. The forces of liberal multiculturalism mobilized and got several people, sympathetic to their position, elected to the school board. The new board overturned the revolutionary idea that American culture (in its true historical application) was, is, or ever will be superior to other cultures. I must simply add that the great flow of immigrants has always headed toward America, not away from it.

Satan has long been a keen observer and a keen student of human nature. In that sense, he is the supreme psychologist. Due to long centuries of observation and experimentation, he has an excellent working knowledge of what makes people tick. He is also the father of much of what now passes for "psychological truth." This truth is now held in very high esteem in our man-centered society, seen almost as a type of secular religion. A young girl who was studying psychology in hopes of becoming a social worker recently asked me why I thought so many people went to pastors for counsel rather than "to professionals." By professionals she meant those who have been inculcated with the principles and tenets of modern man's secular religion: psychology. I told her that maybe it was because people sometimes feel that pastors actually cared about them more as people as a result of their Christian commitment. Christian counsel is also based upon an absolute—God's Word—and not on the changing philosophies of man. The sheer number of psychological schools of thought and psychological approaches illustrate the confusion and instability at its core.

American education has long ago fallen under the sway of the behavioral scientists. Psychology reigns supreme. The goal, of course, of the behavioral scientists is behavior modification. The boys and girls (as the fine captive audience that they are) will be remolded into little New Age, liberal socialists that they should have been in the first place (if their parents had not taught them otherwise; in the typical old-fashioned, reactionary way that sane parents tend to do). Outcome Based Education is designed to rectify that little problem. It is a behavioral scientist's best dream. I am not a behavioral scientist. I'm just a simple, old-fashioned educator and parent, but I can still tell you what the outcome of Outcome Based Education will be: chaos.

Dr. Joyce Brothers, who came to fame in America on a syndicated television quiz show, and who is one of the media darlings in the variegated realm of things psychological, recently shared a brilliant nugget of wisdom with the American public. Her golden insight was that sometimes adultery actually strengthens a marriage. Her claim is that the new freedom in sexual areas which women are experiencing in growing numbers puts them on an equal footing with men. This equality is liberating. Seriously, I ask you, could a person be more wrong?! Well, in retrospect, I suppose that a person could be. That person would be the one who chooses to follow her silly advice. The advantage that Dr. Brothers has, however, is that in a godless society, selfishness sells. People are most likely to be deceived at the point where they most want to be deceived. It is all part and parcel of the fallen human mindset. The most efficient type of deception has always been self-deception. As far as self-justification goes, one simply need look to the pronouncements of noted experts like Dr. Brothers for validation. It all works out nice and neat, except for God. His mind is already made up and He is unmoved by the opinions of experts, the talk show conclusions, the media propaganda, and the opinion polls. He deals in repentance, forgiveness, and righteousness rather than validation, empowerment, and carnal self-esteem.

The current darling of psychology is self-esteem. As it is currently being taught in our society, the idea of self-esteem is a self-defeating idea, a black hole that can never be filled.

Just as there is good cholesterol and bad cholesterol, there is good self-esteem and bad self-esteem. I heard someplace that people need three things in their emotional make-up to be healthy: to have somewhere to belong (somewhere where you are recognized as unique), to be loved and to love, and to do something worthwhile with your life. True Christianity provides all those things. In that sense, it also provides self-esteem. True self-esteem comes from a realization by yourself and by others that you have lived in a laudable way. Francis Schaeffer wrote a book called *How Should We Then Live?* How is it that people should live? The answer to that question is that we should simply live according to God's Word. The result will not be a self-esteem which is based upon exaltation of self, upon a focusing on self.

Psychology instructs us to know ourselves. The Bible, however, never tells us to know ourselves. (Politically correct thought sees self-awareness as a religious condition.) The Book of Jeremiah indicates to us that, unaided by God, we can never really know ourselves anyway. Our job is to know God, for it is in His light that we see light. Only then can we hope to know ourselves as we truly are. (That revelation will usually cause people to realize they actually do need a Savior.) What psychology calls self-esteem is actually disguised selfishness. True self-esteem comes from being loved, not from being told how wonderful we are. Those who are truly loved (loved according to God's definition) also learn to love. I don't recall ever knowing even one child who came from a home where he or she was truly loved, who was not secure. The opposite is generally also true.

Don Feder said, "Our parents and grandparents believed that if you wanted to feel good, you should do good; that if you did rotten things, you deserved to feel rotten. They didn't have our high self-esteem. They also lacked our soaring indices of social pathology." American educators have bought the myth that societal stability comes from healthy self-esteem. Educators "build self-esteem" by mouthing things like "You brighten my day," "I'm lucky to know you," and "You're a good buddy." "American students tend to feel good about themselves and do poorly on aptitude tests."[6]

This is not to say that we should not compliment others. Obviously, we should. The points are that the emphasis of the psychological ideal of self-esteem is wrong and that the results of this psychological quest will be counterproductive. Flattery leads only to deception and the production of counterproductive values such as pride, self-sufficiency, and hate. The bottom line of the psychological goal of self-esteem is based on a lie. People are not by nature good. They are born flawed. Their true problem is not a lack of self-esteem. Their true problem is alienation from God. The road back is the road of repentance, humility, and the grace of God in Christ Jesus. In fact, it is the only way.

Since much of what passes for self-esteem in our society is simply selfishness, I believe that the first step toward a healthy self-esteem is to be introduced to the love of God.

Satan is skilled in areas of deception and temptation. His forte is manipulation and his goal is corruption. Satan appeals in others to the things which worked so powerfully in his own heart: pride, rebellion, and lust. He works to destroy all the qualities and institutions in the lives of people and society which preserve them from his corrupting influence. Thomas Jefferson said that only a moral people can successfully govern itself. Satan therefore works to destroy morality. He has in this pursuit a powerful, natural ally: our flesh. Human beings have born in them an inclination to sin. This inclination can be curbed and controlled only by the ministry of the Holy Spirit, the Spirit of truth.

I believe that the general corruption, devaluation, and debasement of the American culture is a result of the ongoing work of the antichrist spirit. I don't think it is very difficult to prove that there has been a general debasement of culture in America. In the total picture of American culture, we see two ongoing trends. The first is a moving away from things which require thought and intellectual energy. The second is the move toward things which can best be characterized by sinfulness, silliness, and superficiality.

The whole society has become a "Now Generation." Everywhere one looks, one sees the second law of thermodynamics (entropy) at work. Things are not (as New Agers claim) moving toward perfection. They are wearing out, breaking down, and moving toward chaos. I shall cite several illustrative examples of deconstructionism. The ongoing rejection of the cultural heritage of Western civilization is creating a national poverty of spirit. The greatest literature of the Western world is being swept into the dustbin of civilization by an ever-more illiterate populace which has been nourished on television, movies, video games, and comic books. Americans, who have long ago become addicted to mind and heart-altering megadoses of the drug of television, have lost any taste for more challenging (and potentially more fulfilling) pursuits— art, for example.

By way of my own little down-home illustration, I offer this example. Over the years, I have often taught an art appreciation course. It sprang out of my interest in painting in general and from my interest in French painters in particular. Since I teach in a Christian school, I am not restricted by things like a lack of official art accreditation. I have always believed that teaching is as much a matter of the heart as it is the head. I believe that the most effective teachers are those who share from the heart the things that are important to them. This is the way I approached art appreciation. I prepared the subject, gathered materials, and gave it to others as a free-will offering.

I taught my students to recognize the great paintings of the Western world from the Renaissance to modern times. (I cannot resist giving this wonderful example of the absurdity of politically correct thought applied to the world of art. It is the supposition by radical feminists that the famous enigmatic smile of the *Mona Lisa* was the result of some sort of male, probably spousal, physical abuse. It is truly amazing, and also frightening, how this bizarre movement sees everything through their own lens of self deception, and then expects the rest of us to take their deception seriously.) My art course was usually well-received. I always told them, "I am going to culture you . . . like pearls." Of course, I was mostly kidding, but not entirely. I believed it was a worthwhile enterprise for them to know the lives of these artists, the history of the times in which they painted, what they were trying to do, their style, their place in art history, and so forth. Art reflects the times in which the artists live. If you disagree with me, simply look at the age in which we live and then look at modern art. You will be convinced. We have moved from a visual disintegration and fragmentation which chronicle man's alienation from God and from others, to an exaltation of all things vile (the speciality of the tax-supported National Endowment of the Arts [NEA]). The prophet Jeremiah wrote of a society which exalted vileness. God judged that society as terminal. The historian Edward Gibbons listed as one of the symptoms of the disintegration of the Roman Empire a tremendous freakiness of their arts. A major difference, of course, is that in America, the tax payers fund their "in-your-face" enterprise. My point is not simply that art has become debased or that this debased art reflects the debased society in which we live, although I believe those points of view are true. My main point is that what is worthless has been substituted for something that had actual worth. My point is also that under the new rules of the politically correct, studying the great art and artists of the Western world would be fruitless and irrelevant since it would be primarily the study of the lives and works of politically incorrect "dead white guys." (On the university level, literature is being purged of the influence of dead white guys like Shakespeare. If it is studied at all, it is often studied through the lens of false and corrupting philosophies like radical feminism. The new P.C. literature, which is being used to advance political and social ideologies, has exchanged its heritage for a mass of pottage, exchanging something grand for something mean and petty, demeaning the process of education.)

The dreadful revisionism in the teaching and learning of literature and history is robbing American youth of the dignity and strength of their culture, of their vision for the future, and of a source of strength. All things momentary devour things historical, also robbing America of any true notion of heroism.

The approach to the teaching and learning of literature and history in America's current schools (primary through university) is sort of what I call "the Alice in Wonderland approach." It is based more and more on fantasy than fact. It reminds me of one specific character in Wonderland: a dog with a type of broom on its tail. As it went, it erased the tracks it left behind. Like that dog, we have been erasing our own past. America is now beginning to show signs of long-term memory loss, a type of national dementia.

I recently had a history teacher from a public school come and ask to borrow a history book from our Christian school. He wanted to see what we could teach that he couldn't. I thought that pretty well summed up the present state of the teaching of history in America. We still teach "real history" in our Christian academy. So do most home-schoolers.

The rewriting of American history by omission and by the emphasis of people and events which would previously had never been considered important, let alone of primary importance, is an attempt to rob young Americans of an appreciation of their culture. Columbus, the Pilgrims, and a multitude of true American heroes have been sent into academic and cultural exile by the forces of political correctness. The new guidelines for teaching history stress the teaching of history as victimology.

> The guidelines tell America's story as one long struggle of groups pitted against each other—white against Indians and blacks, men against women, capitalists against workers, nativists against immigrants, anti-communists against intellectuals, and so on. But when students view American history only through the prism of group identity, they see a distorted and fractured image. Lost is the sense of what unites Americans, forging one people from many.[7]

The teaching of history as victimology only promotes further fragmentation of American society.

Television, videos, movies, and CDs are giving America new heroes—living monuments to sin and selfishness. The new American heroes are athletes, actors and actresses, and rock musicians, revealing the terrible poverty in our souls. People like George Washington, Ben Franklin, Abe Lincoln, Robert E. Lee, Thomas Edison, etc., have given way to the likes of Roseanne Barr, Howard Stern, Madonna, Michael Jackson, Guns 'n Roses, etc. The ancient Chinese had the unique (but true) idea that the health of the nation was tied to its morality. They also felt that morality can best be examined by looking at the music popular in the culture, for it reflects the currently held values of the youth. If we look at music in America, we can only conclude that American youth have a tremendous taste for violence, rebellion, drugs, sex, suicide, and the occult. I believe that conclusion would be valid.

Many American entertainment heroes have turned political. Needless to say, their views are the antithesis of the Judeo-Christian ethic in most cases. They aren't the only ones, however. Paul Schenck has made the interesting point that in 1990s America, the news and entertainment media have merged. Newscasters have become celebrities in their own right. By this, I mean both mainstream news media personalities and those who specialize in tabloid news. The former use their celebrity status to promote and advance their own political and cultural views and agendas. Their shameless celebrations of the Clintons surely revealed their true colors. Seeing themselves as interpreters and arbiters of the liberal socialist agenda, they seek at every opportunity to "reeducate viewers." Much of this journalistic reeducation is simple propaganda. They jealously guard this right. They also get quite angry when those whose lives they deign to regulate are ungrateful enough to refuse their benevolent ministrations. Peter Jennings, for example, saw the November 1994 elections as a voter "temper tantrum." Sam Donaldson disdainfully dismissed it as "less than a mandate." The bane of the liberal news media and their agenda (from their point of view, not from the point of view of the American public) is the conservative talk show. Rush Limbaugh and many others have demonstrated the power of large talk shows to both inform and inspire American listeners and voters. It has also created a rallying point for those who felt powerless to have any impact on an uninterested and unresponsive federal bureaucracy.

The forces of political correctness regard as a threat and as an inconvenience anything that threatens their monopoly of reeducation. They would much prefer to keep Americans from focusing on important social issues. One way to do that is through tabloid television, which feeds the worst tastes of the American viewing public by glorifying criminality and vulgarity, by making minor celebrities out of a wide range of misfits, criminals, and sinners. It is a devastating force for the devaluating and debasing of the American soul.

David Thibodeaux has written two books on the politically correct movement, detailing their fragmenting influence on society. Their specialty is deconstructionism. They are seeking to dismantle American culture and to remake it. He cites the fragmenting effects of the gender feminists, the Afro-centrist movement, the homosexuality movement, and the multiculturalists. The broad spectrum of American life has been affected by these movements. It is a societal application of what used to be called "Values Clarification" in public education (the father of the current Outcome-Based Education [OBE] plan). The idea of values clarification is to unfreeze the values and ideals of children (to deprogram them), to reteach them, and then to refreeze the new values. It was a simple, blatant attempt at the social engineering which the politically correct movement has introduced into the mainstream and broad spectrum of society, sparing nothing and no one in its attempt to deconstruct society. This is even true of our language itself. It, too, is under attack.

The strange politically correct phenomenon of deconstructionism is highly illustrative of the fragmentation that is going on at the core of our culture. Deconstructionism is an attack upon the structure and significance of our language. (The twin sisters of deconstructionism in this attack are the offspring of multiculturalism: multilingualism and genderism. Although linguistic deconstructionism [which believes words do not have absolute meaning] began in our universities, our secular humanist judiciary is partially responsible for this absurdity. A federal appeals court in California recently ruled that state employees have the right to conduct state business in any language they prefer!) Our judiciary creates new politically correct rights with a dizzying speed. Most Americans would be amazed to know that English is *not* the official language of America. There are currently about 150 languages spoken in America. About 32 million Americans speak some language other than English. Our judiciary has opened the door to the reconstruction of the Tower of Babel: the symbol for confusion and chaos. The final common denominator of Americans will not be English. It will be chaos. A fragmented people is a lot easier for a despot to control than is a unified people. Deconstructionism has devalued and debased not only our language, but the pattern of thinking which is inextricably bound up with our language.

The idea of deconstructionism merits a small digression. The first thing we realize in considering the art of deconstructionism is that secular humanist elitists are masters of obfuscation. They detest the idea of absolute truth so intensely, that they will do anything to hide the fact that such truths do exist. They are like the World War II warships which generated huge clouds of smoke in which they could hide when they came under attack. These people are producing a profound and intense smoke screen with the intention of hiding God's truth from people. R. Emmett Tyrrell, Jr., calls this condition "Kultursmog." The amazing thing is that it seems to be working. More and more people are getting lost in the fog. One of the most serious sins in the land of Kultursmog is to tell people that they are lost in the fog. That violates one of the primary principles of those who choose to live in the dark. Absolute truth is annoying, inconvenient, and well, politically incorrect. Deconstructionists believe that nothing has absolute, universal, or eternal worth, significance or value—neither history, nor cultural tradition, nor religion, nor language—nor anything else. They believe that truth, like beauty, is in the eye of the beholder. When they push that idea to its logical linguistic conclusion, words themselves have no ultimate meaning. By extension, neither do lives. True significance is always personal, local, situational, transitory, and fragmented. Each individual and each group must pursue its own truth, its own bent, its own agenda. Disunity and chaos must then prevail. In times of chaos, the strongest will enforce their will upon the others, usually by violence. This is one of the cardinal tenets of Anton LaVey's Satanic Bible: "The strong shall prey upon the weak."

11

The Debasement of Culture

The Bible is a very historical book. In fact, it is the only book in all of human history which studies history from both ends at once. Leaving aside all the spiritual implications, the Bible is a beautifully accurate story of the history of mankind. At the same time, it is a prophetic book. Prophecy is simply history written before it happens. From Genesis to Revelation, from Creation to the creation of a new heaven and a new earth, across the whole sweeping panorama of human history past and future, we can see, learn, and live God's principles. We can learn from the mistakes of the past. We can even learn from the mistakes of the future.

Let's begin by considering King Solomon. God gave King Solomon great gifts. Solomon received great riches and glory from the hand of God. God, however, gave him an even greater gift than those blessings. He gave Solomon wisdom. Solomon, the writer of the proverbs and the Book of Ecclesiastes, was identified as the wisest man in the world. Solomon, however, had a fatal flaw. Just as his father David had been, Solomon was led astray by lust. Solomon rejected God's specific instructions and warnings and embraced the false gods of the foreign women whom he married. Solomon was without excuse, for God had appeared to him twice, carefully outlining His will for him.

Nevertheless, Solomon followed his own lust, rejected God's specific commands, and embraced the worship of dreadful pagan deities like Milcom, Chemosh, Molech, Ashtoreth, and Baal. Satan used Solomon's foolish infidelity to corrupt the whole nation of Israel. Israel, of course, was only too willing to be corrupted, but Solomon should have known better, for he knew both God and God's will. Solomon's disobedience and poor leadership cost Israel dearly. God removed the kingdom from Solomon's son, Rehoboam. Civil war broke out and the nation was fragmented. This fragmentation was the result of godless, inept leadership.

We learn some interesting lessons from this little story. For one thing, we learn that things in government haven't changed very much through the centuries when appraised through the lens of morality. We also learn that Satan seeks to influence a nation by controlling its leadership and that an immoral (or a moral) leadership can have a tremendous impact on the life of a nation and of a people. It was Thomas Jefferson's belief that only a moral populace could make democracy work, that only a moral populace could govern itself fruitfully. In democracies, we sometimes get the leaders we deserve rather than the leaders we need. In our own nation, godless leadership has also led to a fragmentation and a type of civil war—a war between those who truly worship the God of the Bible and those who have chosen to worship Baal. The fruit of Solomon's disobedience led to the reign of one of the most infamous couples in the Bible: Jezebel and Ahab. I mention Jezebel first because she was the true power behind the throne.

The Bible characterizes Jezebel as a false prophetess, a woman of intense evil and pride, a woman who was involved with witchcraft. In essence, witchcraft is an attempt to gain power by occult means over others, over the environment, and over one's own life. The true goals of witchcraft are power and the ability to control. Satan controlled Jezebel, and Jezebel controlled her husband Ahab. Through him, she controlled the entire nation. In order to confront her evil rule, God raised up a prophet, an obedient man of God, Elijah. The story of their dramatic clash is recorded in 1 Kings, chapters 18-19.

Ahab had instituted the foul worship of Baal and his Canaanite consort, Ashtoreth, in order to please his wife Jezebel. Why would people worship Baal? Why would people who should have known better choose to reject the truth and to embrace a dark and demonic lie? Baal worship has a certain appeal to those for whom holiness has no appeal. Baal worship made no ethical demands upon people. They were required only to adhere to ritualistic worship, a worship which had as its goal the manipulation of its deity in order to provide favor, comfort, protection, and prosperity to the worshippers. It not only made no ethical demands upon those who practiced it, but Baal worship tolerated and promoted sexual immorality, catering to the worst instincts of a debased people. Satan has always used the corruption which comes from sexual immorality to attack and control individuals and nations throughout history. Pagan worship knows no boundaries of decency or morality. It promises freedom but delivers only slavery. Its very essence is to pervert, to consume, and to destroy. Those who give themselves over to it not only find themselves deceived and eventually destroyed, but grow ever bolder and more violent in their efforts to seduce and corrupt others. Satan is using those same techniques in our society today.

Charley Reese said that "Caligula, Commodus, Nero, and the Marquis de Sade would be perfectly at home in the United States of 1995." "There is nothing," he wrote, "and I mean nothing, in the way of sex, sadism, masochism, perversion, violence, bestiality, vulgarity, blasphemy, and plain prurient weirdness that is not available to folks today."[1] The simple truth is that man's heart has not changed over the centuries.

The sex drive is one of mankind's strongest drives. That fact is not lost on Satan, who is an astute student of the human race. He has long realized that sex can be a powerful weapon in his quest to seduce, corrupt, and control the human race.

The human proclivity toward sin is Satan's natural ally. James 1:14-16 advises us not to be deceived. Satan incites the lust inherent in the flesh in order to lead people into sin. (The highly psychologized Western world lends little credence to the biblical definition of sin.) While all sin has a negative effect on mankind, Satan understands the corrupting power of sexual immorality. It deadens the conscience. The biblical definition of sexual immorality includes the sins of prostitution, fornication, adultery, homosexuality, sado-masochism, pedophilia, and bestiality. All of these sins spring from a corrupted heart, a heart filled with the darkness that lust brings into a life. Those who commit these sins corrupt themselves and all those they draw into their sins with them. Rather than facing his sin and turning to a holy God in repentance, modern man seeks only to justify his sin and to demand political protection and general acceptance.

Paul Schenck describes how those who are enamored of the new morality (which used to be the old immorality) seek to solve the sexual problems so prevalent in society today.

> The solution for the problem of sexual sin is not based on any concept of righteousness, but

rather upon the desire to solve "social problems." They repudiate Judeo-Christian morality,
with its stress on chastity, fidelity, self-control,
and responsibility. Instead the solutions are
abortions, Norplant, condoms, and the acceptance of homosexuality.[2]

In the case of homosexuality, for example, man
seeks not only to justify his behavior, but to insist that
others recognize it as normal, that it be taught in our
schools, and given legally protected status by our courts.
Their strident rejection of godly righteousness (and of
those who take a godly stand against their sin) grows
daily, reminding biblically literate people of Genesis
19.

There is, of course, always a price to pay for sin.
The Bible says that the wages of sin is death; spiritual
death and sometimes physical death. That is the light
in which we should see the present AIDS crisis—the
black plague of the modern world. This modern plague
would be preventable were it not a politically correct
disease. Linda Bowles said that AIDS has become a
platform for the promotion of the very behavior which
spreads it.

History has taught us that Satan is scarcely ever
original. He doesn't have to be. He just sticks with
what works, though of course he makes very efficient
use of technology.

There is a medical apparatus which is sometimes
used in the treatment of cancer. It is a type of pump
which is affixed surgically to the patient. This small
pump administers ongoing doses of chemotherapy
around the clock. Chemotherapy is actually a type of
poison which kills the cancer cells. Unfortunately, it
also kills healthy cells. It would be insane for healthy
people to have such a pump affixed to them. The
American entertainment media is likewise delivering
an ongoing dose of poison to those who are hooked

up to it. There is a cumulative effect to the treatment. It induces cancer of the soul rather than curing it.

Sex is clearly one of the primary products being sold by television and movies. I was watching an old film by Kirk Douglas the other day. I mean old. It was about as old as I am. It was interesting in many ways because it was produced in a by-gone era for a movie audience that no longer exists. It also reflected the morals and mores of that time. In that sense, it was sort of a video historical document. In this film, Kirk Douglas' character learns that his wife had a baby out of wedlock before they met. He was devastated! So was she! The tone of the movie left no doubt that it was something she saw as terribly wrong and painful. Immorality had a clear definition then. It had consequences. People were ashamed of it in their own lives and offended by it in the lives of others. That theme doesn't translate very well into a 1990s context. Except among the older generation, premarital sex and illegitimate children have little or no stigma. In many inner city situations, it is a badge of maturity. It is also the door to getting a financial handout from the state. The concept of sin has evaporated. Of course, once the understanding of sin evaporated, the concept of any true repentance also evaporated. Repentance is often the only way to true growth. Self-justification only gives birth to more "self" things, like self-indulgence. Growth of character then becomes more and more difficult.

Sometimes I try to look at television with the eye of a person who was born in the 1940s rather than the eye of a person whose sight has been dulled by living in the 1990s. The Bible identifies the eye as a gateway to the heart. In 1990 America, the eye in the case of most viewers is not governed by a moral governor, by a sense of morality, let alone by common sense. There is no moral voice (call it conscience) which says, "This is wrong. Don't watch it." By dint of repeated exposure to the new morality (packaged in a variety of means), the uncritical viewer begins to see sin as normal. This is especially true of younger, vulnerable viewers, viewers who do not have an historical perspective.

Popular sitcoms paint immorality as normal and desirable; and humorous. The popular shows depict premarital sex as a given, as an "everybody is doing it." It is not administered like castor oil, but rather like something sweet to the taste, dressed up in humor. It becomes very palatable and slides down very easily, a far cry from my old Kirk Douglas movie.

The great historian Edward Gibbons listed an unhealthy preoccupation with sex as one of the major factors which contributed to the disintegration and collapse of the Roman Empire. We live in a sex-saturated society. We have made an idol of sex in America. (Amazingly, liberals continue to cry out for more "sex education," which has been proven to promote promiscuity, as well as a rejection of both common morality and decency. What was introduced into American schools in the 1960s as sex education is sexual proselytizing in the 1990s.) It is the primary tool which Satan is using to undermine the moral fabric of American society. Once again, history shows us how Satan revealed his character and agenda through specifically chosen vessels of evil.

Hitler had no morals in the traditional sense of the word. Satan is a pragmatist. Hitler was also a pragmatist, using what worked best at a specific time in order to implement his plan. He was an expert at debasing the consciences and the characters of all those who submitted to his will. He was an expert at creating co-conspirators. Hitler, for example, outlawed abortion for Germans and officially opposed homosexuality. The "prodeath camp" in our culture stridently portrays those who stand against abortion as being the heirs of Hitler. They are painted as those who would impose their morality on others. You cannot actually ever impose morality on people. It is a matter of the heart. If you could, however, it would be better to impose morality than to oppose immorality—which is what the secular humanist camp is attempting to do under the banner of "freedom." Hitler opposed abortion because he needed many, many young children to be fed into his death machine as living sacrifices. German children belonged to the state. They were educated to kill and to die for Hitler. Hitler, a totally morally degenerate person himself, opposed homosexuals for purely practical and political reasons: they can't reproduce.

Once Hitler conquered a nation which he considered to be fit only to be the slaves of the master race, he promoted homosexuality and made abortion readily available among the conquered peoples. It was both a means of population control and a carefully planned activity whose goal was the moral corruption of the population. Hitler worked toward the goal of searing the conscience of the nation, toward a cultural debasement. Hitler said that he came to set people free from the "poisonous folly of morals and conscience." Hitler promoted pornography among the conquered peoples. He also promoted alcoholism and prostitution. These things were weapons for him. Those who could not be seduced were intimidated or eliminated. It is standard operating procedure for dictators to destroy the intelligentsia of the nation.

Hitler saw the concentration camps as the supreme weapon of terror and intimidation. At first, however, they were simply called "reeducation centers." Hitler was a master of euphemism—as are dictators and governments with something to hide. The skillful use of the euphemism is an important step in the battle for the truth. The first step in attacking the truth is to redefine it. Hitler learned that the key to having people accept a redefinition of the truth is constant repetition.

That is, of course, a task best performed by the media. In America, sin is constantly being redefined. Homosexuality is "an alternative lifestyle," abortion is "the freedom to choose," pornography is "sexually explicit material," profanity is "explicit language," and so forth. Hitler also used the German courts to give new definitions, to give new rights, and to deprive people of former rights.

The Communists used the principle of reeducation with devastating success in both the Soviet Union and China. Washington is also making excellent use of the reeducation principle (often called sensitivity training) to advance its agenda in areas like AIDS education, diversity training, the promotion of homosexuality, gender feminism, and so forth. Those who have no inclination to be reeducated, illuminated, or sensitized, face various sort of penalties: reassignment, firing, fines, etc. People who now are being ostracized and penalized, will one day be criminalized as those who have rejected the new cardinal tenets of society: relativism, diversity, and toleration.

Once the moral base of a people is destroyed, it is easy to control them. Hitler corrupted and controlled German education, using it to advance his agenda. He also controlled or eliminated the intelligentsia of the nation, a tactic used by Stalin, Mao, Pol Pat, Saddam Hussein, and others. Hitler did not want a population which could think. Their job was simply to obey and to serve until death. It was a case of "dumbing down" the nation—academically and morally. (This, by the way, is the true face of O.B.E.)

The Nazi regime illustrated how technology can be used to totally control a nation. Clearly, Hitler could have been much more effective at promoting his agenda if he had had the tremendous resources available for the job in 1990s America. Sadly, we don't need a Hitler. Hitler was used by Satan to establish a debased moral climate in Germany. We are doing it to ourselves. America, once the major exporter of the gospel around the world, has become the world's largest exporter of both materialism and filth. Filth, of course, is an equal opportunity enterprise. There is, in the human condition an innate drawing toward sin, a weakness which is constantly exploited by the media, desensitizing people. The domestic machine for filth and violence is kept running at a fever pitch, fueled night and day by American television, American movies, American magazines, American fashion, and American videos. Filth is a major growth industry. As Pogo, the noted philosopher said, "We have met the enemy, and he is us."

The dearly departed paragon of leftist absurdity, Jocelyn Elders (who accurately portrayed the elitist view), campaigned stridently for sexual liberation in America, insisting that America is "sexually repressed"—a view shared by people who hate the idea of godly absolutes and by those who love immoral behavior like pigs love slop. In truth, however, America is anything but repressed. America is saturated with sex. What those who glory in their immorality are really attempting to do is to attack and eradicate traditional morality in the name of "personal freedom." This rearrangement of the facts is not a new technique. E. Michael Jones wrote a book called *Degenerate Moderns: Modernity as Rationalized Sexual Misbehavior*. In this book he asserts that much of modern thought has been shaped by people like Freud, Kinsey, and Mead, whose assaults on traditional morality were motivated by their own moral degeneracy. His conclusion is that there are ultimately only two alternatives in the intellectual life. "One either conforms desire to the truth, or one conforms truth to desire." America is choosing the latter path. During one of the proliferating demonstrations for "gay rights," a reporter asked a national gay rights advocate what the demonstration was all about. In a candid admission (not for national media consumption) he admitted simply, "It's about sex."

The debasing of the American culture (which is a planned activity), the propagation of immorality, violence, and filth show no signs of letting up. Like Rome, we are collapsing from within, imploding under the pressure of the moral vacuum which we have either created, or which we have permitted Satan to create. The process has been slow, steady, and cumulative. It has also been effective. Our society now totters on the edge of moral collapse, a moral collapse somewhat like the economic collapse in 1929—the collapse which inaugurated the Great Depression. The Great Depression was both devastating and worldwide. The spiritual collapse will also be devastating and worldwide, plunging the world into a new Dark Age, into a new age of paganism.

12

Christianity as a Counterculture

The dictionary defines *counterculture* as "a lifestyle that is opposed to the current culture." The greatest counterculture figure in history has always been Jesus Christ. That was true during the time of the Roman Empire. It is still true. Jesus is the greatest countercultural figure of all time, not only because He has been irreconcilably at odds with both the secular authorities and the religious establishment, but also because He brought the culture of heaven to earth. Jesus, who is truth incarnate, was filled with compassion but devoid of any compromise—an incomprehensible combination to a world which is short on compassion but long on compromise.

Culture is defined as the "customs, beliefs, ideas, practices, etc. of a given people in a specific time period in history." Cultures change. They blossom and they also fade. The strength and the dignity of the American culture has historically been a heritage of all that was best in Western civilizational thought. Its true greatness was drawn from its powerful Judeo-Christian heritage. That has changed. America has exchanged its spiritual heritage for a bowl of pottage. Charles Colson, echoing Francis Schaeffer, has written that we are now living in a post-Christian era. Our nation grows not only more un-Christian each year (from a biblical point of view), but clearly more anti-Christian. As it was at the very beginning, as it was in the early Church, Christianity (true biblical Christianity) is once again becoming a counterculture in a pagan world, which is, by turns either apathetic or antagonistic toward it (just as it was in the time of the Caesars).

The aged Apostle John was sentenced to the bleak island of Patmos by the Roman emperor Domitian. Domitian, who hated Christianity and Christians, no doubt assumed that John would soon collapse under the heavy toil of digging and transporting the gravel which would serve as the basis for the famous Roman roads. Tradition says that John carried a basket of gravel on his back up and down the steep and rocky paths on Patmos. Domitian no doubt assumed that he was in fact giving John a sentence of death. John, however, outlived Domitian and was off Patmos in two years or less.

John was on Patmos because he was not willing to acknowledge Caesar as Lord. John would only call Jesus Christ his Lord. Rome was a multireligious society, bound together by the worship of the emperor, who supposedly incarnated the essence of Rome. The Roman emperors were held to be divine. Even their portraits on a coin were regarded as holy. Roman law more or less permitted people to pursue peacefully their own religions as long as they were willing to burn a pinch of incense to Caesar once a year and to affirm that Caesar indeed was Lord. It was a nice situation for those who were lukewarm and for those who were willing to compromise their beliefs. John, of course, was not such a man. By refusing to worship Caesar, he identified himself as a traitor to Rome, a man who merited death. To reject Caesar was to reject the state itself, since Caesar was the true incarnation of the state, uniting in his person both divine and secular authority. He was the superstar of the superstate. It was high treason to reject the lordship of Caesar.

Many Bible scholars believe that the letters to the seven churches in the Book of Revelation (chapters 2 and 3) represent the entire scope of the Church age from Pentecost to the Rapture. They believe that each church symbolizes the state of the church at a specific time in world history. That idea may or may not be true, but it does give us a basis for a consideration of the Church throughout world history.

The first two churches which were mentioned (Ephesus and Smyrna) took strong doctrinal stands in the midst of an immoral and idolatrous world. Ephesus supposedly represents the apostolic church. Smyrna represented the persecuted church; a persecution sponsored by the Roman emperors. During all that time (from approximately A.D. 33 to around A.D. 300), the Church existed as a counterculture in a totally pagan world. It maintained a witness and a testimony to the love, light, and life of Christ Jesus despite pressures from without and pressures from within. The Greek word *thlipsis*, which is used in reference to the church of Smyrna is a word which indicates the grinding oppression brought to bear on it by a godless world. The church at Smyrna refused to compromise, patiently enduring suffering. This, in fact, is precisely what makes Christianity revolutionary in a world dedicated to personal fulfillment, success, and individual wealth and power. The very name Smyrna suggests their lot in life. Smyrna meant "myrrh," a substance which was crushed in order to be used in funeral proceedings. When crushed, however, it gave off a sweet savor in society (2 Cor. 2:14), a sacrifice to God.

The Church was unmoved by oppression or bloody persecution. It grew only stronger and more pure, maintaining a powerful witness and testimony in society. I see it rather like a spiritual fur ball caught in the throat of society. It had to be either expelled or digested. The best efforts to expel the Church had not worked. Society decided therefore to digest it.

The Church had grown used to its very unenjoyable role as outcast and underdog. The situation (described in the third church in Revelation 2) abruptly changed in the reign of the emperor Constantine.

At that time, Christianity was only one of many religions in the Roman Empire. Constantine, for reasons of his own, decided to send it to the head of the class, elevating Christianity to the position of official state religion. With that elevation came official favor and protection. The Church, which had survived every pressure which the world had brought to bear against it, suddenly found itself tested in new ways; by comfort, prestige, glory, and gold. The Church felt that it had "finally arrived." The body of Christ, which had been born in humility at Pentecost, began to become an institution rather than a living body, spiritually united to its head, Christ Jesus.

As the life flow was pinched off (John 15), the Church began to wither spiritually (although it prospered physically and politically), and it lost its witness of life, light, and love. Constantine erected a beautiful new church building in A.D. 314 (the first official church building), which would display and showcase Christianity as the official state religion. Constantine himself became the head of the Church, once again uniting Church and state, as was the case in pagan Rome. The third church in Revelation is the church of Pergamos. Pergamos means "mixed marriage." When the institutionalized church was digested by the world system, it lost its counterculture role in society. Some individuals, however, remained true to the Lord. It is they who held the testimony of Jesus Christ and kept the flame of Christian counterculture burning in society. Although the Church would go through revivals and relapses throughout the coming centuries, those individuals who would "remember and repent" continued to function as salt and light in society. They were overcomers. That scenario has continued up to our own times where the true church of Philadelphia is being spiritually separated from the worldly, apostate church of Laodicea.

It is now the church of Philadelphia which maintains the counterculture witness in society. Philadelphia is not a denomination. It is neither a coalition nor an association. It is not a worldwide council of churches. It is the worldwide body of Christians which belongs to God's true church—the church which holds faithfully to the testimony of Jesus Christ and the Word of God. This church is not great (as men see greatness), rich (as men see richness), powerful (as men see power), or loved by a "politically correct" world which esteems all the things that the church is not. We are living in a society which has lost its road map. The response of this society, however, has not been caution. Instead, it has been an overconfident acceleration, a careless stomping of the accelerator. Our society is now wildly careening toward disaster.

In a growing flood of evil, which has been picking up steam since the end of World War II, sin, relativism, the toleration of sin, and the love of sin have seemed to bury the Judeo-Christian ethic. I say "seemed" because God has remained in control. As Christianity has become less and less the spiritual center of American culture, it has become not only a countercultural force but the hope for our nation. The prophet Jeremiah spoke of a time when people called evil good and called good evil, a time when "vileness was exalted among men." That society was declared terminal by God, judged, and punished. We are now seeing the same cultural condition being duplicated in our age.

I believe that God is raising up people who will stand out in the growing darkness, as those described by the prophet Daniel as "shining brightly like the stars and leading many to righteousness" (Dan. 12:3). Although there has always been a price to pay, God has never lacked for counterculture heroes throughout the church age. The Greek word *martyr* is the same word as the Greek word *witness* (Rev. 12:11). The churches of Smyrna and Pergamum had two such heroes. The bishop of the church of Smyrna was the venerable Polycarp, a disciple of John. He was arrested in his eighties and ordered to declare Caesar to be Lord rather than Jesus. Polycarp, who had lived his life in the light, love, and life of the Lord, refused. He was burned to death, praising God.

I recently saw a football coach on television who said that his team won because it "had played all sixty minutes," maintaining a vigorous effort until the end. That is also expected of Christians. We are called to a commitment, and we are expected to maintain that commitment until the end. As Paul said, we are to run the entire race if we expect to win the prize. Polycarp did. That is why Polycarp was a counterculture hero.

In Pergamum, Antipas stood firm for Christ, even in a domain where Satan ruled. *Antipas* means "against all." He refused to compromise and stood fearlessly for righteousness, even to death. Tradition teaches that Antipas was burned to death in a brazen bull during the reign of the emperor Domitian. Domitian had boasted he would destroy Christianity. History has proven that he was overly optimistic, due in part to the sacrificial example of men like Antipas. The Church still needs those who live Revelation 12:11.

I sometimes think that opinion polls are to be greatly feared, especially in an age which has lost its spiritual compass. It seems that one can validate (or disprove) almost any position by taking a poll. Although

I do take the results of polls with a grain of salt, they can still sometimes be a valuable measuring rod in our society. Having said that, I now say this. In a recent poll, it was determined that 18 percent of Americans have what they consider to be a "totally secular viewpoint." It was also determined that about 19 percent of adult Americans take their faith seriously enough to practice it with regularity, faithfulness, and depth. Eighteen plus nineteen makes thirty seven. That leaves 63 percent somewhere in the middle. It is to be supposed, however, that the great majority of the 63 percent are much more influenced by the viewpoint of the 18 percent than they are by the 19 percent. As T. S. Eliot said, "Paganism has all the valuable advertising space."

Every day we see more clearly the truth of the axiom that "in order for evil to succeed, it is only necessary for good men to do nothing." It is past due for the good men and women who are among the godly 19 percent of our population to take a stand. (God was willing to spare Sodom if he could find ten righteous people.) How should they begin? Cal Thomas has observed that the more one knows about and is committed to the teachings and principles of one's faith, the more one is likely to oppose efforts by the less religiously committed (or uncommitted) to promote policies that contribute to the undermining of the social structure. He also feels that the small number of committed people are not likely to change the political climate of our secular-humanist-pagan culture by political activism. The best, primary, and most fruitful investment of their time may be to teach others the essentials of their faith. Morality rests upon religious commitment. American Christians must invest their time in spreading the Gospel of Jesus Christ. The most obvious place to start would be where one is. Logically, that will most likely mean in the home, in the schools, in the work place, and everywhere else God opens a door.

For a Christian, both presumption and pessimism are sins. The former indicates an overconfidence in the flesh. The latter indicates a lack of faith in the wisdom, power, and love of God. There has never been a perfectly Christian nation. There can also never be one due to God's very precious gift to the human race: free will. Within every time period and within every nation, God finds people whose hearts are hungry for two things: the truth and a true relationship with Him. Those people become a sort of "living Bible," bearing witness to God's desire and ability to change the lives of people. Those who are changed have a testimony which may be ignored, but which cannot really be either disproved or discounted. The legacy that these people leave to the world is the fruit of a Christ-centered life. Their witness is the power of God to change lives. This redemptive theme runs through the Bible from Genesis to Revelation like a scarlet thread. That is the message of the Church: the Good News. That is the reason that the Church cannot be pessimistic. Its eyes and its hopes are not upon man. They are focused upon God who is firmly and totally in control of the historical process, both for individuals and for nations.

God has a threefold plan. He will rapture the Church. At that point our job will be done. He will raise up the Jews who will finally receive Jesus Christ as their Messiah to preach the gospel throughout the whole earth. I once heard somebody say that one day soon one simple question will reconcile all the differences between Judaism and biblical Christianity. That question for the Jew will be, "Lord, were you here before?" The final segment of God's plan is that He will judge the nations of the world. Until the Church graduates, our hope will remain the same for both the Jews and for the nations of the world: revival. Revival is the true atomic weapon of the Church. Does God graciously give revival or does the Church "pray it down"? I believe that the two possibilities are actually one.

13

The Constitution Yesterday, Today, and Tomorrow

Since the U.S. Constitution is the hinge upon which our understanding and application of justice, liberty, and civil rights swings, I think it is worthwhile for us to take a brief look at what our Constitution was intended to be, what it now means in our modern secular society, and what it is likely to become in the future.

In order to fruitfully proceed in our little study of the Constitution, I think it is important for modern Americans to disabuse themselves of the notion that our Constitution was written by a group of primitive, unsophisticated, out-of-date colonials. The truth of the matter is that they were a truly amazing group of men— a group of some of the most intelligent, committed, and astute political thinkers ever assembled at any time in world history. They were steeped in the historical traditions of justice, liberty, freedom, and human dignity. They had a thorough understanding of history, law, philosophy, and theology. Above all, they understood the human condition, the human heart, and their impact on the mechanics of politics and government.

The Roman historian Tacitus chronicled the lives of the Roman emperors. Tacitus, who was an "insider" in the dangerous days of the emperor Domitian, came to distrust power and to understand its potential to corrupt. In this observation he agreed with Lord Acton who also wrote of the corrupting influence of power—especially absolute power. Our founding fathers were well aware of the writings of Tacitus. They were also well aware of the works of distinguished political writers like Locke, Montesquieu, and Blackstone. Although they often quoted these men, they were four times more likely to quote Scripture. It was this healthy fear (based upon a true understanding of the human heart) that motivated our founding fathers as they sought to set specific limits on centralized government power as they wrote our Constitution.

Jefferson, who spoke of "binding men with the chains of the Constitution," understood two important things: true freedom is based upon law, and man's natural inclination is toward evil. These men thus set out to write a political document which would not only define and protect the values and traditions for which they and their countrymen had fought so ably and nobly, but which would remind them that their new republic had been forged within the parameters of divine providence. The Constitution which they produced was the crowning jewel of Western political thought. Thomas Jefferson called the U.S. Constitution "unquestionably the wisest ever yet presented to man." "William Gladstone, one of Britain's greatest prime ministers called it 'the most wonderful work ever struck off at a given time by the brain and purpose of man.' "[1] These men were speaking at least as much from their Christian world view as they did from their political acumen. Our Constitution shone most brightly in American history during the years when our nation rejoiced in its Christian heritage.

Although the politically correct revisionists have done everything they can to rewrite American history in order to convince modern Americans that our country was founded as a secular society, their position is based on a blatant falsehood. Clinton's plan Goals 2000 was proposed to implement a national curriculum—including the teaching of American history. The proposed teaching of American history is divided into thirty-one specific "standards" to be mastered. Not one of these thirty-one standards mentions the Constitution. It is, of course, one of the key theses of the humanist manifestoes of 1933 and 1973 that America is a secular society—a society which can be characterized by a rejection of the Bible, Christ, and salvation—a society built upon human reason, evolution, technology, the global community, and human autonomy. The historical truth, however, about the founding of America was that

> The concept of a secular state was virtually non-existent in 1776 as well as in 1787, when the Constitution was written, and no less when the Bill of Rights was adopted. To read the Constitution as the charter for a secular state is to misread history, and to misread it radically. The Constitution was designed to perpetuate a Christian order.[2]

In the specific case of those who were drawn together by political necessity and by the hand of Divine Providence to write our Constitution, I think that the whole was greater than the sum of the parts. Why?

> Most of the delegates were committed Christians with a love for and knowledge of the Word of God, men who included God in their thinking in all affairs, particularly those of government. Even if they weren't committed Christians, they reflected to a man the Biblical phi-

losophy so prevalent in their day. It would have been impossible for these men to fashion a Constitution that wasn't based on Biblical principles, for they represented their own principles of life as well as the convictions of those citizens who would ratify and implement the Constitution.[3]

The distinguished gentlemen who gathered in Philadelphia clearly represented the thinking, aspirations, and religious values of the citizens in 1787. Although this was not a religious conclave, the overwhelming number of the delegates were of such religious belief and character as to preserve this document from including any principle that was contrary to the Bible—which nearly all held in high esteem. Besides, they knew they must have it ratified by all the states, all of which were strongly Christian. It wasn't popular in 1787 to be an infidel in America.[4]

The framers of the Declaration of Independence understood that man's inalienable rights are not derived from the intrinsic worth of man. They are derived from the dignity given to man by his creator. (Of course, in this day and age, what the Founding Fathers called "self-evident truths" are no longer quite so self-evident.) Our Founding Fathers accepted the biblical account of creation. They were, of course, "unenlightened" by Darwin's theory of evolution. (Can you imagine the possible response Darwin and his followers might have received when they related the news to George Washington, Thomas Jefferson, Benjamin Franklin and all the rest that they were descended from apes and that they were themselves simply a species of higher animal?! Uh huh.)

Historically, America's religious heritage and America's constitutional heritage are absolutely entwined. In truth, the two are inseparable. They will stand together or they will fall together. This is what prompted Lynn Stanley to write that "Americans get off the fence and make a bold stand for righteousness." The idea of taking a righteous stand is a scriptural one. The Book of Jude urges Christians to "contend for the faith that was once and for all entrusted to the saints." Christians must be in the forefront of calling America to return to its constituting truths and values.

Domestic crises are a fruitful ground for the gaining and the expansion of political power. Whenever centralized power grows, the intrusion of government into the lives of the citizens also grows. Linda Bowles made the point that "a vast centralization of power came under Wilson and Roosevelt. They had world wars and a Depression to deal with. Afterwards, the power stayed in Washington, turning eventually into LBJism."[5] Washington became a type of power magnet. The Supreme Court, which had been instituted as an additional check on the power of the federal government by the Founding Fathers, became instead part of the Washington power structure. The secularizing influence of the Supreme Court has been due in large part to their promulgation of the theory that the Constitution is an evolving document. In other words, the Constitution no longer means what it used to. The original intent of the Founding Fathers is now deemed to be irrelevant. The Constitution now means what the Supreme Court judges decide that it means in light of twentieth century social realities.

How did the central principle of the Constitution get stood on its head? The chief villain was Franklin D. Roosevelt. His New Deal didn't just "expand" the power of the federal government, as is usually said; it destroyed the very principle of resistance to federal expansion. From then on, the federal government has had the power of writing its own constitution. In 1940 Roosevelt's rubber-stamp Supreme Court declared the

10th Amendment a mere "truism" of no force or effect.[6]

Joseph Sobran said that

> since Roosevelt, the federal government has had any power it wants to claim. Rooseveltian progressives saw the Constitution as a fatal obstacle to socialism. Roosevelt's revolution was to eliminate the guiding principle of the Constitution to limit federal government. Unfortunately, most Americans now believe that upholding the Constitution means submitting to the Supreme Court.[7]

Were it not for the 10th Amendment, our founders would have never ratified the Constitution. (The 10th Amendment stipulated that the powers which are not specifically given to the federal government belong to the state government and the people.)

> They correctly feared the development and consolidation of a powerful and meddlesome federal government. Our federal government has reversed James Madison's understanding of government. Madison saw the powers delegated to the federal government as few and well defined. The present state of government is that the powers of the federal government are numerous and indefinite, and those of the states are few.[8]

The 10th Amendment has been functionally nullified.

The goal of the ever-expanding growth of government and the centralization of power is to insure that the power elite will ever more effectively be able to impose its will on those who are being governed, the same class of people who are paying the bill. In order for the One World Government ideal (which is the ultimate in rule by a power elite) to be feasible, America must be politically restructured. The One World Government concept is the bottom line of what we have come to know as the New World Order. It cannot happen unless America is restructured by the New Age ideal. In order for America to be restructured, the U.S. Constitution must be nullified.

In the course of the many radio programs I have done on my various books, I have had a few people make the point that they fear people like Pat Robertson (and other Christians) because they "want to change the Constitution." Sadly, they do not realize that our Constitution has already been changed. Men like Pat Robertson just want to change it back to what it was. The New Age movement/New World Order/One World Government crowd rely heavily upon the fact that most Americans have lost any significant historical perspective. Most Americans have little liking, appreciation, or understanding of American history. Modern life emphasizes all that is temporary, spontaneous, and fragmentary. In this endeavor, the forces of the politically correct serve as a type of deconstructionist SS, attacking the integrity of Western tradition wherever they find it. Their ultimate aim is to produce chaos, a chaos which will necessitate the emergence of rule by a power elite. It is in this light that we can best see how our Constitution is under attack.

I have already indicated that the U.S. Constitution is being constantly reinvented by the Supreme Court. There has been talk recently of reopening dialogue on the Constitution. Some favor specific amendments, passed through Congress by the usual legislative process. Others favor constitutional conventions in the individual states. Given the moral, spiritual, and political climate in our nation at the present time, either initiative (but especially the latter) could prove disastrous to our constitution. It may all prove to be a moot point, however, if some sort of actual, fabricated, or perceived national emergency requires the president to rule by executive order under a martial law situation. That mechanism is already in place under the

FEMA provisions. In the event of a serious national emergency (foreign invasion, domestic insurrection, terrorism, economic collapse, etc.) the Constitution will be suspended, and the president will assume a leadership role which was never granted under the Constitution. We saw a similar situation in Russia when Boris Yeltsin dissolved the Russian Parliament in a time of national upheaval and assumed direct control. Of course, in his case (as well as in ours) the opposite could also have been true; a military coup of the government would have also led to a suspension of their constitution.

Most Americans naively assume that a military coup would not be possible in America. William T. Still, author of *New World Order: The Ancient Plan of Secret Societies*, wrote in his book of a secret plan to use military force to keep Nixon in power as his political hold on the presidency was crumbling. Having thoroughly investigated the entire matter, he still concluded that

> the most plausible theory is that some sort of timetable was in place, and then someone got a little anxious to eliminate Constitutional government as we know it in the United States. They not only significantly overestimated their own strength, but the forcefulness of the reaction to their plans.[9]

George Bush already established the principle of bypassing the U.S. Constitution by means of an American treaty with the U.N. Our involvement in the Gulf War was an example of that application. We can conjecture that in the case of a worldwide emergency, nations (including ours) might choose to reject the idea of national sovereignty, electing to submit to the leadership of a worldwide governing body.

In May 1994, Bill Clinton signed a presidential

directive which asserted his authority to place U.S. military forces under the operational control of a foreign commander, a clearly unconstitutional transfer of power.

It is, therefore, neither accidental nor incidental that in 1964, 76 percent of the people trusted the government to do the right thing most of the time, but only 19 percent do today.

> The belief is widespread that the power to make their own decisions and control their own lives has been unconstitutionally taken from the people and transferred to bureaucrats. Every problem in America, every human need is used as an excuse for the confiscation of private wealth, the suppression of individual freedom and the expansion of an already bloated government bureaucracy.[10]

The Progress and Freedom Foundation recently did a poll where half the respondents said that they foresaw a time when they may have to oppose the law in order to protect and preserve some of their constitutional freedoms.

14

Courting Disaster

In the courts of ancient monarchs, royal jesters provided comic relief. These jesters cavorted about, making people laugh (especially the king) with their amusing antics. In America, members of the judiciary have become a type of jester king in their own courts, uniting authoritarian power and capricious behavior, somewhat like the mad queen in *Alice in Wonderland*. But nobody is laughing.

In Carroll's famous tale a normal little girl falls head over heels into a mad world, ruled by a mad monarch. It is an absurd world which does not operate according to any sane rules. Everything worked only according to whim and whimsy. Poor Alice never knew quite what to expect since the rules were always changing. *Alice in Wonderland* conveyed in a humorous fashion what it is like to live in an absurd world. Since it is (at least on the surface) a story for children, it lacks the impact of the novels of Franz Kafka. There is nothing humorous about the confusion, disorientation, and frustration of Kafka's characters as they seek to make sense of all that is happening to them, as they seek to find their way in a world where all the familiar moral and intellectual landmarks have either disappeared or have been rearranged. The frustration of both Alice and the characters in Kafka's novels remind me of the American legal system. The familiar traditional legal indicators, landmarks, and signposts have somehow disappeared, to be replaced by the whim and whimsy of humanistic situation ethics. Cut adrift from the anchor of its historical legal ethics and precedents, American justice is adrift.

The spirit and the substance of the law has been violated by the rejection of godly absolutes. Since ancient times, the law has understood and practiced the simple principle that virtue was to be rewarded and crime was to be punished. According to that simple equation, people could be held accountable for their actions. The Enlightenment changed the way that people thought. Man-centered rather than God-centered, people saw the causes of society's problems and the solutions to those problems differently. The Enlightenment caused what the New Agers call a paradigm shift in the perception of reality. "Much 18th century thought considered human nature essentially good. Crime thus became the fault of society. It followed that you produce good people by reforming society."[1] This flawed belief has been one of the pillars of Western secular humanistic thought. It has also been one of the guiding principles of our humanistic court system. Supreme Court Justice Clarence Thomas (a voice of sanity and reason) said,

> If people know they are not going to be held accountable because of a myriad of excuses, how will our society be able to influence behavior and provide incentives to follow the law? An effective criminal justice system cannot be sustained under conditions where there are countless excuses for violent behavior and no moral authority of the state to punish.[2]

Having divorced itself from the true basis of law (godly absolutes), the Supreme Court has decided to remake society in their own humanistic image. Our judiciary has become capricious and arrogant, regarding itself as the true basis for law. The law is now what they say it is. The Supreme Court is playing according to the same principles in our legal system that the Kinsey report promulgated in American sexual affairs. Kinsey decreed that "sexual right and wrong depend only on what most people are doing sexually at a given moment of history." In other words, godly absolutes are out and situational ethics and preferences are in. Sociology (the study of how people relate to people) has become the establisher of right and wrong in society. Modern law has become sociological law. It is law which reflects the modern views that there are no absolutes and that the Constitution of the United States can be made to say whatever the courts of the present want it to say based on a court's decision as to what the court feels is "sociologically helpful" at the time. Historically, it has never been the responsibility of the Court to set social policy, but to faithfully make decisions based upon the bedrock of Constitutional law.

Charley Reese writes that

> screwball situations arise when judges make decisions based on ideology and social fads rather than on law. The law, properly, is a reflection of a moral code. But when the law is perverted to achieve social or ideological goals, it frequently becomes immoral.

Reese goes on to give examples of this screwball justice.

> In Florida, a woman may abort her baby, but if she uses crack while she's pregnant, she can be charged with child abuse. Another young woman shot herself in the abdomen while pregnant and

has been charged with murder. In Florida a
school nurse cannot give a child an aspirin for
a headache without written permission from the
parents, but the child can get an abortion—a far
more serious medical intervention, to use the
jargon of the trade—without notifying her parents.[3]

American justice is both a *symptom* of what is happening in American society and a *contributing* factor to
what is happening in American society. Deprived of
absolutes, court rulings become ever more preposterous, ever more absurd, as both judges and jurors make
new rules. Psychology has done its job well—convincing
American judges and jurors that nobody is ever really
responsible for his actions. In the resulting climate of
conclusion, it has become increasingly more difficult
for twelve jurors to agree on anything. It is the judicial
age of Menendez, Bobbitt, and O.J. Simpson.

Justice in America has clearly lost her way. When
the citizens of California had the audacity to exercise
their political right and to express their desire to cease
funding the lives of illegal aliens in California (Proposition 187), a strident elitist cry went up immediately.
The voters were not only called racists, but were also
taken to court by their own government officials—who
were presumably elected or appointed to represent the
people and to uphold the law. They did neither. What
they did do was to reveal one of the most heartfelt
beliefs of liberal elitists; that American voters cannot
be permitted to decide such issues (issues which have
major impacts on their daily life) unaided, unguided,
and unopposed.

Voters in California simply wanted the immigration laws enforced. Instead, they were informed that
they were not politically correct enough in a scenario
reminiscent of the political theory postulated in the
satirical novel *Animal Farm*, where all the animals were

equal, but some were more important than others. In this interesting turn of events, we see several cherished American beliefs targeted for the junkheap in the New World Order: patriotism, American sovereignty, democracy, local self-determination, an appreciation of Western culture and civilization. In an even more amazing (but also revealing) turn of events, Mexican and Latin American authorities protested the position of American citizens in California.

> Newly inaugurated Mexican president Ernesto Zedillo has put out in the open what was once covert policy: The Mexican government relies on heavy immigration north of the border to take care of its underclass, shifting the burden to California taxpayers.[4]

The presidents of Mexico, Guatemala, and El Salvador all bristled with outrage that Californians voted for Prop. 187, seeing fit to lecture America on human rights violations, a supreme irony in the case of Guatemala and El Salvador. They were so upset because they have come to see America as a dumping ground for the unemployed. William Booth of the *Washington Post* writes, "Central American countries in particular rely on emigration to relieve destabilizing pressures at home, while aiding their economies through remittances sent from the United States."[5]

There are currently more than two million illegal Mexican immigrants living in America. The millions of Mexican immigrants in our southwestern states is drastically changing the culture there. (That is the cherished desire of elitist multiculturalists.) The multicultural elitists hate American culture, American sovereignty, and American patriotism.

Christopher Lasch wrote,

> Members of the elite have lost faith in the values, or what remains of them, of the West. Many

of them have ceased to think of themselves as
Americans in any important sense, implicated
in America's destiny for better or worse. Their
ties to an international culture of work and
leisure—of business, entertainment, information,
and "informational retrieval"—make many members of the real elite indifferent to the prospect
of national decline.[6]

They see immigration (both legal and illegal) as a
way to accomplish their purposes. As examples of what
is happening I cite the attack by Hispanic activists on
the Alamo as a symbol of white American domination.
I cite the erection of a statue in San Jose to Quetzalcoatl,
the bloodthirsty Aztec divinity. The followers of this
pagan deity worshipped him by offering him human
sacrifices whose hearts had been torn from their living
bodies. Quetzalcoatl is quite a role model! His twenty-
five foot high statue (which cost the taxpayers a mere
five hundred thousand dollars) stands as the antithesis
of everything represented in traditional American culture. In Arizona and Florida, Hispanic activists are
seeking to legally implement a resolution that English
not be recognized as the official language. The courts
in Dade County, Florida, caving in to the pressures of
multiculturalism, have given the right to a local cult to
indulge in blood sacrifice of animals.

It is no secret that America has been either unable
or unwilling to control its illegal immigration problem.
Illegal immigration is an assault on several concepts in
which Americans have traditionally believed: the importance of true national sovereignty, patriotism, a
healthy respect for American culture, and an understanding of America's uniqueness and its godly mission. Illegal immigration stands more and more for the
opposite of those values.

America's elegant *Statue of Liberty* symbolized what
America meant to the world in the days when every-

body (Americans included) prized what America stood for. Immigrants from all over the world brought skills, talents, abilities, and hope to our shores. It was their intention to become Americans, to make a new life, to make a contribution.

> Years ago immigrants of all ethnic backgrounds worked diligently to become "Americans," learning English and moving into the national mainstream. But this is not the trend today. Ethnic blending is out; ethnic separateness is in. Many non-Anglo Americans seek to retain and use their native languages and perpetuate their native customs, effectively making their communities outposts of their mother countries.[7]

Early immigrants parroted Patrick Henry: "Give me liberty or give me death." Things have changed. "Today's communism-indoctrinated immigrants are likely just to say 'Gimme!'" Andrew Kawecki said, "Early immigrants came to the United States for freedom and democracy. Today's immigrants come here to get rich, and they don't care how." "This attitude is expressed in many ways—the most devastating and ominous of which is the great number of illegal aliens who are involved with organized (and unorganized) crime."[8] Justice cannot remain uncorrupted in a society which has rejected godly absolutes, in a selfish society which no longer knows right from wrong, good from evil. World War II can in some ways be characterized by the Holocaust and the bombing of Hiroshima. The Supreme Court dropped a secular humanist A-bomb on the morality of our society in their Roe vs. Wade decision. The fallout of this American holocaust will be properly measured and evaluated only in eternity.

In *Roe vs. Wade*, the Supreme Court legalized murder of unborn children and overturned the laws of forty-nine states. Tony Snow, who calls *Roe vs. Wade* a "breathtakingly shabby piece of jurisprudence, a political act in pseudo-constitutional raiment," explains that "in the view of the Supreme Court, the right to privacy extends to sex and abortion—and nothing else."[9] We shall look at this dreadful American reality in the next chapter.

15

The Debasement of Education: An Educational Perspective

It is my belief that our nation has been rejecting the true basis of the American culture. In doing this, we have also been rejecting the source of our strength, our vitality, our greatness, and our historic mission. We have been embracing a new world view; a false world view which is built upon materialism, relativity, multiculturalism, and politically correct thought, a view which in a historical sense is anti-American. The profound changes in our culture can best be understood by looking at the current state of the institutions which are redefining American culture: the government bureaucracy, the courts, the media, and the schools. Since I have been a professional educator for thirty years, and since I have some well-founded opinions on the very important topic of education in America, it seems like an excellent vantage point from which to consider the culture war.

Germany's defeat in World War I was followed by the Great Depression of 1929. German currency became so devalued that it literally took a bushel of

German bank notes to buy a loaf of bread. The devaluation of Germany currency wiped many people out.
They had labored all their lives for money which no
longer had any value. There is presently a cultural
devaluation going on in America. This devaluation is
evident in American education. Some of our nation's
most precious cultural resources were spiritual, not
financial. It might be argued, in fact, that the elevated
American standard of living is traceable to its rich
spiritual and cultural heritage. The very things which
were at the heart of American culture, the things which
were the basis of American strength and genius are
now being devalued and replaced; just as American
silver dollars were replaced by paper notes, just as
silver quarters in America were replaced by quarters
formed of base metals. There was a medieval belief
that base metals could be changed into pure gold by a
process called alchemy. We in America have reversed
that process. We have been turning spiritual gold into
base things. That has clearly been the trend in American education.

In the colonies, the schools were originally religious in nature and in purpose. Even as the school
grew more and more secular with the passage of time,
it was still understood that a godly world view was the
norm. Schools were heavily influenced by the Protes-
tant Puritan ethic: belief in hard work, patriotism, integrity, honesty, law and order, morality, obedience to
God's authority and to authority in general, respect for
others, duty, and godly character. I am sure that as you
read that list of what American education once was,
you are asking yourself "What happened?!" What happened was the dramatic secularization of American
education.

In the 1940s through the 1960s the idea of permis-
siveness dominated American child-rearing. It was in
this period that psychology became deified in America

and began to remake the schools. Americans who had been educated to believe that salvation (both corporate and individual) was to be found only in God, were reeducated to believe in the supremacy of man and in his problem-solving abilities. The key to salvation became not God, but education. The fuel that fired the engine of education in America was money. The solution to all of the problems of society was more money for more education. Unfortunately, divorced from godly absolutes and godly morality, all the money in the world cannot change the nature of man. The problem has never been in man's head; it is in his heart. Only God can change hearts. American schools have thus become something different than they were designed to be. That is why they don't work. That is also why American public schools have helped spearhead the entrance of our nation into the present secular age—an age which is both "post-Christian" and in many ways "post-American" (at least according to the original vision of America as penned by our founding fathers). Control of American education is an absolute necessity for the secular humanist power-brokers. Without this control, they cannot hope to succeed. Hitler summed it up best by saying, "He who controls the schools controls the future."

We can thank Jimmy Carter for making this task easier for the educational elite. Carter created the Department of Education. This creation made government control of public education much easier and much more complete. It also made American public education largely the fief of the NEA, a political organization disguised as an educational organization. The primary interest of the NEA (the most powerful lobbying group in America) is to expand its already considerable power and to establish an educational monopoly. It works diligently to raise teacher's salaries (thus maintaining a highly satisfied membership which will not object to the radical NEA ideology). Sadly, many American public school teachers have been beguiled by the siren song of the NEA: greed. They have been convinced of a new educational philosophy which can be summed up by the credo: "we want, we need, we deserve!" The escalating power of the NEA corresponds more or less exactly with the decline of academic performance in American public schools. The NEA supported Bill Clinton's presidential campaign quite vigorously, knowing full well that his political views corresponded closely with those who are at the helm of the NEA. The NEA, of course, loves the idea of Clinton's Goals 2000 which calls for the loss of local power to govern the public schools, the introduction of a national educational bureaucracy, and a national curriculum. It is much easier for the NEA to influence the federal government with its power lobbying ability than it is to influence fifty individual states. The sad state of educational affairs which will one day soon be rued under the initials of OBE is already being presaged by the fact that although student performance and student enrollments are declining, the number of administrators and nonteaching staff is growing. The outcomes of Outcome Based Education (OBE) will be decreased performance, increased costs, and the implementation of a radical secular humanist agenda.

"Public education," of course, is a misnomer. Public education is actually "government controlled education." The government controls what it funds. Unfortunately, for those who rejoice over this consolidation of the hold of the educational elitists, they must still deal with both private schools and with the ever-growing phenomenon of home-schooling; educational institutions which thwart the secular humanist monopoly. Private Christian schools and home-schoolers are hard for the government to control because they are not vulnerable to financial pressure from the federal government.

Education for Christian schools and home-schoolers is a matter of principle, a matter of commitment, a matter of discipleship. The educational establishment must therefore seek to combat Christian schools and home-schoolers by legal means and by an ever-expanding propaganda program. The very words *school vouchers* are enough to send liberals into paroxysms of rage. The supporters of "the right to choose" evidently limit that right to the aborting of children, not to educating them. The truth is, however, that school choice is only social justice. The rich have always had it. They can opt out of the public school system while forcing others to remain imprisoned there. (It is to be understood, of course, that Christian schools must never trade their freedom for school voucher money. If vouchers come with conditions that will lead to more government control over private education, they must be rejected.)

Many Americans have been rather thoroughly propagandized in matters educational, although I think more and more people are catching on. I believe that more and more people are sensing the poverty of spirit behind secular humanism. Secular humanism is the official religion which is practiced and taught in the public schools of America. A good farmer knows quite well what he hopes to produce. He does not plant weeds simply because they are so easy to grow. Americans should be as wise as the farmer. They should closely inspect what American schools are producing. They should also closely inspect what American schools are designed to produce. American schools are, in fact, designed to produce secular humanists. Cal Thomas calls public education "the farm team for the next generation of liberals."

Since it rejects the idea of godly absolutes, secular humanism can never unify our nation, unless, of course, the secular humanists find a way to win the culture war and to eliminate all the true (practicing) Christians and every vestige of authentic Christianity. (*Authentic* means "true to its definition." That definition is strictly based upon the Bible as God's revelation of truth.) Morally speaking, the secular humanist agenda, currently being taught through our public schools, will prove to be devastating to our youth and to our nation. People who have long been concerned about the academic "dumbing down of America," are now beginning to see the fruit of the moral dumbing down of America. The two go together. Walter Williams described the academic situation in America by saying that

> in 1930 only three million older Americans couldn't read, compared to today's forty million. The National Adult Literacy Survey reported that among adults with twelve years of schooling, over 96 percent couldn't read, write, and compute well enough to attend college.

Williams added that "only 56 percent of black people over the age of fourteen could read compared with 80 percent in 1930. In 1990, it was estimated that 40 million young Americans with nine to twelve years of education couldn't make sense out of a printed page."[1] Cal Thomas illustrated the diminishing of American morals by saying, "In fourth grade my class began learning fractions and how to find the lowest common denominator. Now students find the lowest common moral denominator."[2] We in America have sown the wind and reaped the whirlwind. What has happened to America? Don Feder says that

> human nature hasn't changed. People were just as covetous, lecherous, and violence-prone in 1954 as they are in 1995. Teens were every bit as rebellious and hormone-driven then as now. The difference? Society changed all of the red lights to green lights. Once we taught sexual restraint through our schools and popular cul-

ture. Now we teach indulgence. Once we taught personal responsibility. Now we teach that if you do something despicable, it's everyone's fault but your own.[3]

Charles Colson summed it all up by saying that "the crisis is not political. It is moral and spiritual."[4] "Today's Western culture rejects absolutes and enshrines only self-indulgence."[5] "We are witnessing the most terrifying thing that could happen to a society: the death of conscience in a generation of young people."[6]

That truth has already become painfully evident. This agenda will accelerate the slide toward national fragmentation. I believe that this is what it is designed to do, at least by the true inventor of secular humanism, Satan. He has long been using the educational elite toward his own ends. Their pride makes them easy prey for Satan. This elite has always seen public school education as the proper vehicle to remake society, to produce a secular millennium. Their grandest efforts will ultimately only produce the chaos that Satan covets. Just as righteousness can never come from sin, unity can never come from chaos. Revelation 6 teaches us that in the end, every man's hand will be turned against his brother.

There was recently a round-table discussion on television between some assorted liberals and conservatives on the subject of education. One of the conservatives made the point that American schools are failing because they provide no coherent or worthwhile moral base. A liberal spokesman smugly replied that he had been in a school just the other day and proudly announced that he had seen written nice and large on the blackboard the statement that "We must respect each other." "That," he announced "is teaching morals." The first speaker then made the point (to applause from the audience) that it is easy to invent

slogans and put them up on posters for all to see
without any intention or ability to live up to the poster.
Such slogans often tend to lose something in transla-
tion.

In this arena, things are often not what they seem.
In order to comprehend in this day and age what
things really mean, people must be sure to translate
them in the light of our current culture. The "We must
respect each other" statement may well (and probably
does) mean "toleration"—one of the most sacred beliefs of New Agers. Toleration really means "Don't try
to tell me that there are absolutes. You have no right
to tell me that anything I do is wrong. What is right for
you may not be right for me. Your job is to be open-
minded, tolerant, and accepting."

Unfortunately for them, however, there are absolutes—God's absolutes. Human beings may be absolutely sincere and yet absolutely wrong. Christians (by
biblical definition) cannot be tolerant of sin or error.
Before leaving on their great spiritual adventure, the
Puritans were known in their native lands as non-con-
formists. The current negative reputation that they have
in American history is based largely on their intolerant
stance toward sin. Sin, of course, has been redefined in
our society. It is (in our politically correct Brave New
World) no longer considered doing wrong, repugnant,
or unrighteous things. It is being intolerant of those
who are doing these things. It is like a giant, national
game of "Let's Pretend." It is a living illustration of
Psalm 2.

If the Bible is correct that "righteousness exalts a
nation" and that "sin is a disgrace to any people" (and
I have every confidence that it is), the promulgation of
the humanistic ideal of tolerance may be one of the
greatest sins of all. Our society badly needs people who
will stand up boldly during this battle for truth and tell
people that the "emperor has no clothes on." Unfortu-

nately, those people will not come from American public schools. They are also not likely to come from politically correct American universities. I called this chapter the "Debasement of Education." To *debase* means "to make lower in value, quality, character, or dignity." I believe that this is exactly what is happening to American education. Founded upon the ideal of promulgating the truth in American society of the Judeo-Christian ethic, our schools are now dedicated to the ideal of opposing that ethic in society. William Bennett said simply that education is supposed to make people smarter and better. Our system of education is guaranteed to do neither.

"To educate" comes from the latin word *educare*, which originally meant "to bring up, to rear, or to train." Those who are Bible literate will no doubt be reminded of Proverbs 22:6. The Proverbs give God's view on education. They were written as an educational manifesto for the children of Israel. Proverbs deal with concepts like knowledge, understanding, wisdom, instruction, and discipline. Proverbs is a very practical book, a book of principles by which people can successfully live in the here-and-now, a book of wisdom which will affect their eternity as well as their present. Two of the key principles of the Book of Proverbs are that the fear of the Lord is the true beginning of wisdom and knowledge and that God holds parents primarily responsible for the education, training, and upbringing of children. God is quite clear on the point that children are a gift from the Lord, that He has given them to parents to raise to know Him; that He has not given them to the state. In this, God agrees with William Bennett: education is to make people smarter and better.

16

Hang Down Your Head John Dewey

I am sure that you have played the game "connect the dots" sometime in your life. If the person playing the game does it correctly, the connected dots eventually form some sort of a picture. I think that we can form spiritual pictures in the same way, by playing connect the dots using people. I believe that it is clear that both God and Satan have used key individuals throughout history to implement their opposing plans. To see the picture that the Satanization of society is forming in America, we need only isolate key individuals in strategic societal areas who have worked to oppose God's plan; and to connect them. The picture which emerges spreads across the breadth and depth of our society. It is also an ever-expanding picture which covers the past, the present, and which projects itself into the future. We can easily connect dots like Marx, Darwin, Freud, and Dewey into a humanistic overlay on society. Dewey is the largest educational dot in the history of modern American education. Since much of the current culture war is being fought on the educational front, I think it is worthwhile to take a close look at Dewey, to see how, where, to whom, and to what he is connected in the educational picture.

The *New World Dictionary* lists John Dewey as "an American educator and philosopher, exponent of the pragmatic approach to education." Knowing what I know about God's opinion of the wisdom of this world, I am naturally suspicious of anyone who is officially labelled a philosopher. Dewey's pragmatism was of a Hegelian variety, excluding any emphasis on biblical morality and ethics, choosing to stress and to implement a policy where the rights of the individual are absorbed by the state. This same Hegelian-pragmatic approach prevailed in the Weimar republic in Germany leading to the expediencies of euthanasia and mass murder in Nazi Germany, illustrating that amoral pragmatism can sometimes be lethal. Within the Nazi system, the extermination of the Jews was not a moral issue. It was seen as a pragmatic attempt to find a final solution to the "Jewish problem."

John Dewey sought to introduce the theory of William James, a noted American psychologist, into American education, thus forming part of the headwater of the psychological theories which now inundate American education. Pragmatism, like most things which are theoretical and speculative, myopically concerns itself only with "everyday realities," dismissing the possibility of any spiritual reality. Pragmatism judges success simply by results. Long before the advent of all things psychological, the Bible instructed us that we are indeed best able to judge things by their fruit.

Although the theories of John Dewey have had an enormous impact on American education (and thereby on American society), judged by its own definition, pragmatism has been a costly failure, both academically and morally. Seen from God's point of view, Dewey and his pragmatism have been weighed in the balance and declared to be featherweights. But to be fair, I must give the devil (and Dewey) his due. Dewey was very successful in beginning the process which has led to the secularization of American schools. Dewey's fondest secular humanist dreams are now a reality in American public schools. The secular humanist agenda can best be characterized by the following ideas: the promotion of abortion; an acceptance of homosexuality as normal; a redefinition of the family; the teaching of evolution as scientific truth; the deification of psychology; a soft academic curriculum; the promotion of globalism; the rejection of godly absolutes; a specific exclusion of the Judeo-Christian ethic in all forms and practices; sex education courses; the rejection of Western culture; the nationalization of education; globalism; etc.

John Dewey was the first president of the American Humanist Society. The Humanist Society was (and is) committed to the restructuring of society, along socialistic lines. Dewey, whose primary impact was on American education, was in some ways typical. Being the good humanist that he was, Dewey rejected the holy God of the Bible, the biblical plan of salvation in Christ Jesus, and the existence of sin and eternal absolutes. Dewey also rejected the idea of traditional morality, choosing to believe instead that morality is relative to changing conditions and needs in society. For Dewey something was "moral" or "true" only because it worked. He felt that truth was subjective and personal rather than fixed and absolute. Truth was to be found within rather than from above.

Like all good humanists, Dewey had an unfounded faith in the problem-solving abilities of mankind as it moves merrily on its way to a secular millennium. John Dewey appeared on the American educational scene at a time when powerful societal forces were reshaping a society which was growing ever-more secular. It was an age in which mankind was beginning to have faith in three man-centered approaches to understanding and ordering modern life: evolution, psychology, and sociology. Dewey was confident that mankind was finally on the brink of establishing its own secular millennium—a perfect new world in which everyone would live happily ever after, free from the demands of a holy God. In this belief, Dewey joined hands with other secular heroes like Darwin, Freud, and Marx. (A secularist seeks to banish God. A humanist seeks to enthrone man in His place.)

Dewey saw education as the proper tool to accomplish his goals of secular humanist social engineering. In a statement filled with candor and with vintage secular humanistic philosophy, Dewey said that the primary reason for the existence of public schools was to remove the "irrational religious influence" that the children might otherwise retain from their parents. It was thus that the system of values clarification was born. Values clarification seeks to "unthaw" formerly held beliefs in order to reteach and then to "refreeze" them. Dewey thus saw education as a means through which a humanistic elite could redirect the process of education. Education would be a type of indoctrination in the process of "socialization" of students. The bottom line of socialization is the formation of global citizens, an idea revered by the socialist Dewey. Dewey felt, in fact, that the socialization of children was the primary function of American public schools. Socialization is a process by which students are molded to fit the needs of the state. Clearly, the idea behind Dewey's socialization was to produce small, compliant cogs for the grand elitist machine.

Since Dewey held nothing to be eternal, sacred, or absolute, his interest and energies were devoted exclusively to affecting life in the here and now; an ominous idea in the light of fallen mankind's selfish nature. This is, of course, one of the defining characteristics of diehard secularists. They are without an eternal perspective, totally time-bound and earth-bound. Dewey, who rejected the idea of traditional authority (i.e., religion, family, tradition), opened the door to educational chaos. Chaos is often not an accidental fruit, but a planned activity. The dictionary defines chaos as "a state of utter confusion."

All legitimate authority is based on God's authority. God's authority is a bulwark against the spiritual forces in the universe and the very laws of nature (beginning with the Fall of Man) which are constantly moving everything toward breakdown, dissolution, and disintegration. Despite what the secular evolutionists claim, nothing in the physical universe (including people) is moving toward perfection. Instead, things are breaking down. Science calls this the second law of thermodynamics (entropy). Once God's Word is rejected, chaos is guaranteed. The introduction of chaos was Dewey's most significant contribution to education.

Dewey, who is often called the father of progressive education, was actually the father of permissive education. Since Dewey's main interests were in the process of socialization, his approach to education was primarily non-academic. (This makes him the grandfather of the current Outcome Based Education movement.) The curriculum was not "book-centered," but "activity-centered," the polluted spring which now feeds the process of the "dumbing down of America." A student of the silly educational theorist, Jean Jacques Rousseau (whose greatest personal educational achievement was to send his own children to an orphanage to be educated), Dewey believed (or pretended to believe) that children were born with a desire to learn by doing. They needed only the freedom to develop naturally. He felt that children should therefore decide for themselves what is worth studying. This idea implies that the great cultural tenets of Western civilization are not really very important. Neither are our traditions. This is the legacy given to America by John Dewey, the global, multiculturalist deconstructionist.

Dewey believed that the truly socialized child must establish his own curriculum, must establish his own educational pace, and must serve as his own motivator, evaluator, and disciplinarian. (Anybody who has spent more than ten minutes teaching will no doubt get a big chuckle out of these notions.) The classroom teacher was to serve as a guide and a facilitator, helping open up the paths in the life of the students of preexisting inclinations. I presume that one such preexisting inclination is that play is always more fun than work, therefore more desirable. This idea has come home to roost in the OBE system where teachers are to be politically correct psychological midwives, who will begin guiding students into their "own inclinations" at the earliest possible moment and away from more academic pursuits. In the end, however, their inclinations will actually be those of their benevolent facilitators, and psychology will provide the carrot and/or the stick.

Dewey's approach to education was to involve children with ongoing problem solving (within a peer group context) which would serve to "clarify values" away from the Judeo-Christian ethic. (Christians, however, whose values have already been clarified by God, will be like strangers in a strange land in this system.) Education will be highly technological. Grades, tests, competition, and knowledge (as it traditionally existed in schools) will be outdated concepts which will be replaced by an electronic dossier. Dewey thus began the "anything goes" approach to education which inaugurated the "dumbing down of America." Thus began the spiritual vacuum presently existing in American schools which so many negative forces are seeking to fill these days. To you, wherever you are these days, I say, "Hang down your head, John Dewey!"

17

On the Cutting Edge of Absurdity

Perhaps you are aware that there is an educational elite in America. This group is a subgroup of the larger cultural elite group. They are educational specialists. This group has worked long and hard to put our nation on the cutting edge of educational absurdity. What does this group want? They want what elitist groups have always wanted: power. They pretend, of course, that they will use this power for the good of all those nonelite types who are deemed incapable of running their own lives. They may even believe in their own good intentions, illustrating that the most effective type of deception is always self-deception.

You have no doubt never personally met a member of the educational elite. You may wonder why not. You may wonder where it is that they can be found. The educational elite live high among the clouds in the land of smoke and mirrors. Even if you could visit them in their rarefied atmosphere (for they have no intention of coming down to your level), you couldn't communicate with them, because they speak only two languages: edu-speak and globaloney. Their needs are simple. All that they require is for you to unquestioningly do their bidding. They live in condolike ivory towers, high above it all, looking down now and then through their telescopes at all the educational serfs who are faithfully cultivating their little gardens on the educational flatlands. Although they themselves would never get their hands dirty in such mundane enterprises, they are convinced that their innate superior intelligences and their time to cogitate upon matters educational will enable them to remake the lives of those who live below.

Fortunately for them (and unfortunately for all the educational serfs) their avocation is the same as their vocation: tinkering. They just love to tinker. They are sort of a type of tinkering educational royalty. They share this in common with Louis XVI, who was also a noted French tinkerer. Louis loved to work in his little royal tinkering shop. Actually, he was quite good at it. Unfortunately, he wasn't very good at being king of France. He tinkered his way right into the French Revolution.

Sometimes tinkerers also have revolutionary impacts on society—negative revolutionary impacts. As our own nation is slowly beginning to realize, when revolutionary processes go too far, it is hard to reverse them. It is rather like trying to unfry an egg. American liberals have been working for about seventy-five years to undermine American society, to strip it of the glue which held it together: the Judeo-Christian ethic; and to replace that ethic with many wonderful and amazing new politically correct ideas and ideals. The measure of their success can be clearly seen in the disintegration of our society. Oh well. No problem. All that is required is more tinkering. Unfortunately, the tinkering social engineers are unable to tinker a way to get the evil genie back in the bottle once they have set it free upon our land. I thus accuse them of equal parts malice and stupidity.

Any social engineer worthy of his certificate of malice and stupidity, however, knows that in order to remake any civilized society, it is imperative to control and to remake the educational system. It is important to be thorough, cumulative, and progressive (historically an important word for all those in educational ivory towers). The new progressive educational buzz phrase is "a world class education." The obvious goal is to control the educational process from top (graduate schools, universities, colleges) to bottom (nursery schools). The fruit of their educational tinkering has always been negative. It will continue to be. As proof of this, I offer the educational theories of John Dewey: the new math, the new reading (whole language), the academic courses without any academic substance, the new politically correct studies, the open classroom, and finally, OBE (outhouse based education . . . er, I mean outcome based education). OBE is the crowning gem of educational chaos and control. It isn't actually a new idea, but it is an idea that the social scientists believe a deluded and desperate society is ready to receive. It is the ultimate tinkering—not an adjustment to a former system, but a totally brand new system.

Have you ever gone for a ride on a very steep and menacing roller coaster? It chugs slowly to the top, and as it does, the implication of what is about to happen suddenly dawns on you. At the very peak, you may well wonder if you really do indeed want to go on this trip. But, alas! It is too late. Our educational roller coaster has chugged to the top of its cycle and is ready to plunge the nation into a wild ride of chaos which will end in disaster.

Perhaps the most important question we should ask ourselves about the educational tinkerers is this: "Why do they do it?" True to the spirit of our educational enterprise, I shall give you a multiple choice test.

A. They simply love to tinker.

B. They do it because they are bored.

C. They tinker because they honestly believe that education should not be left to the unenlightened. (The unenlightened would be simple, hard-working classroom teachers, parents, etc.)

D. They have other reasons—reasons which they are either unclear of themselves, or if they are aware of these reasons, don't usually care to discuss them with the educational serfs.

E. All of the above.

The correct answer (as you probably already guessed) is E. The results of their educational tinkering, however, are always the same. They promote dissolution and chaos and always serve to weaken education.

By way of illustration, I will limit myself to discussing two examples: the "whole language" approach to reading and the open classroom. I will comment more fully on the ultimate masterpiece of educational tinkering (OBE) later.

Before exploring the new philosophy of the teaching of reading which is being promoted in our public schools, I shall ask you to consider this semi-rhetorical question: "Why do you suppose that the ivory-tower educational experts want to implement a system which they know will not work?" (This is only a semi-rhetorical question, because I plan on giving you the answer.)

But first a little background. There are two approaches to teaching children to read. The first is the phonetic approach. Children learn to sound out their language phonetically enabling them early on to master the mechanics of their language and to make reading open-ended. They can sometimes go far, fast. But slow or fast, they actually learn to read. The other method is the "whole language" approach. It is also sometimes called the "look and say" method. Children approach English sort of like it is Chinese. That is to say, they learn individual words as ideograms, memorizing each new word separately, and guessing at words they don't know.

So, then, why do they do it? Why are they resolved to introduce a system into education which will lower academic performance? Why teach a system of reading that guarantees that a large number of students will never learn to read? The answer is twofold. The whole language approach is politically correct, a tinkerer's delight. That alone might be reason enough. The New World Order folks love everything which is of a holistic nature, where all the segments fit nicely into a New Age (holistic) whole.

In that light, the other answer makes perfect sense. The other reason would be at least partially economic. Both reasons would be based upon a New World Order social agenda. The educational bureaucracy feeds on itself, creating an ever-larger monster. Children who fail at reading can be categorized as having "learning disabilities" and placed in special programs, generating additional bureaucratic jobs, and bringing in extra monies from educational agencies (which the taxpayer indirectly funds). Of course, new programs always require new textbooks, new materials, new paid experts, new teacher training programs, new testing agencies, and so forth. By now you are probably seeing the giant dollar sign which is superimposed on a system of reading which is designed to fail.

Students who are designated as "special education" candidates in any way are always relatively defenseless in our system of public education. They are largely at the mercy of the educational machine. In order to be peacefully and fruitfully recycled, they must at all costs be compliant within the program. No compliance, no carrot. The fact that it was the system which facilitated the failure of the student in the first place, is a fact which has been lost in the process.

I am, therefore, forced to wonder if those in the educational ivory towers ever wanted our public schools to succeed, at least in the way parents want them to succeed. (Keep in mind that a large percentage of the educational elite send their children to elite private schools.) Eliminating academic and moral excellence at every turn, they guarantee a chaos which will serve to necessitate the dictatorship of those in our schools who wish to use them as indoctrination centers. Psychology and cults agree on the proper methodology to do the job. One first works to destabilize existing structures. The result will be confusion and chaos (sometimes called "creative disorder"), which will facilitate the establishment of a new structure, a new paradigm.

They have been practicing that theory within the classroom for years under the name of values clarification. If that is truly their goal, they obviously consider it a drawback if students: A) know how to read B) like to read. People who read tend to also be people who are not easily deceived, people who are not easily led astray and managed by the process of social engineering. They have a window upon history. Those are at least a few of the reasons why "Johnny can't read." Johnny, of course, often doesn't mind being deprived of the ability to read in an entertainment-oriented culture like ours. Reading, writing, and thinking are often, dare I say it?—work. Meanwhile, Johnny's parents are often too busy to notice. The homeschoolers both notice and do something about it; one of the reasons the social engineers both fear and hate the home-school movement and the idea of school choice. It would largely spell defeat for their fondest tinkering hopes.

I have a modicum of personal experience with the open classroom. Before I share my experience, how-

ever, I must tell you that although the open classroom
is a terrible idea, a school which is composed of all
open classrooms is a terrible idea squared. The individual open classroom can be somewhat contained and
its influence minimized. An open school is like a bee-
hive gone mad. The best you can hope for with a
flawed idea is to apply it perfectly. Unfortunately, even
with a perfect application, the result will still be confusion and chaos. Although the idea of the open classroom is wrong-headed at its best, and thereby guaranteed to be a disaster, there is even a "wronger" way to
apply it. (I realize wronger isn't actually a word, but in
this case, it just somehow fits.) Of course, I did understand that the theory behind the idea of the open
school was to integrate and coordinate the various academic disciplines into one unified, holistic approach
where teachers and students could relate and communicate as one fruitful, happy community. Happily,
however, the teachers in the public school where I was
semi-gainfully employed for a season, didn't want to be
integrated or coordinated. They primarily wanted to
be left alone.

Once we (by "we" I don't really mean the teachers,
but rather the educational overseers who were in charge
of the plantation) made the decision to pursue the idea
of the open classroom, the die was cast. The teachers,
who generally have a common sense view of matters
educational, almost universally rejected the idea. I have
no idea why "we" chose such an apparently silly approach to the building of a new school. Perhaps it was
just the temptation of being educationally chic. (This is
a tremendous temptation for some administrators.)
Perhaps there was some other reason. Perhaps there
was no reason. At any rate, the powers that be decided
that they were at least minimally obliged to make a
token effort to convince the faculty what a splendid
idea it all was. So the secondary school staff was trundled

off in buses to visit a nearby "open school." The idea, of course, was to inspire us to greater educational heights. So we dutifully toured it, talked to a few folks, and came home again, shaking our heads and chuckling to ourselves over the overwhelming preposterousness of the plan. And thus, our new school was built.

Our new school was built largely without interior walls. There is a famous line of poetry by Robert Frost that says, "Something there is which doesn't like a wall." That wasn't true in our school. The teachers made a valiant but vain effort to build walls the best they could with whatever materials they had at hand: bookcases, filing cabinets, etc. I personally was thrice blessed. I had a room with three walls. The *piece de resistance* of this folly was one large warehouselike room which housed six classes. Since my room was next to the big room, I had plenty of opportunity to observe its functioning. Sometimes it was comical. Whenever a teacher or two did something of an audio-visual nature, it sounded like "Dueling Banjos." Sometimes it was, well, I am not sure exactly what, but I could hear six voices droning on, discussing six unrelated, uncoordinated subjects. I can only conjecture on the sum total of the mass educational experience, but I can testify first hand that frustrations, frictions, and aspirin sales went up tremendously. Predictably, the great experiment failed. In the fullness of time, real walls were constructed wherever feasible. In the meantime, there was plenty of nice chaos for everyone to enjoy.

Perhaps the best known line ever written by the prolific English novelist, Charles Dickens goes, "It was the best of times. It was the worst of times." That would sum up the question of vouchers in American education. It would be the best of times for American education—specifically for students and for their parents. It would be the worst of times for all those who are stubbornly holding onto their vested interest in the educational monopoly presently stultifying American education. It would introduce the principle of competition and free enterprise into American education. It would also bring about both responsibility and accountability—things which the presently entrenched educational powers fear, despise, and dread. The consumer (for in truth, that is what students and parents are) would finally have some leverage.

Nearly everyone has had a frustrating experience with some branch of government bureaucracy. They can be arrogant and obnoxious in their dealings with the public simply because the average citizen has no recourse but to submit to them since there is no other choice. The IRS is the living proof of this. Monopolies breed complacency, arrogance, and inefficiency. They discourage accountability. The federal government is forever making noises about parent involvement in education. (In case you are wondering, thus far they have just been kidding.) The absolute best way to actually do that is to give parents direct control over their own expenditure in the educational markets. Most Americans are canny shoppers. They are very likely to learn quickly how to get the best deal for their money. But alas, that is exactly what the federal government greatly fears and cannot permit. It would derail their program of social engineering, the nationwide values clarification program which it hopes to implement.

Values clarification is an attack on godly absolutes. It teaches (as John Dewey believed) that truth is only personal and situational. One of the great undergirding principles in this secular belief system is "toleration" of all truths which do not endorse God's absolute truth. The end result of that, of course, will be a belief system which, by believing everything, believes nothing. "Toleration of diversity" is the driving principle behind multiculturalism. The latter is a lie which is built on a lie, for no truly multicultural society has ever succeeded in world history. Any system which lacks cohesion in its core is doomed to self-destruct. This system of thought will only magnify and accelerate all the problems of society which are already to be found as a microcosm within the schools.

As the truth about what is actually happening trickles out, the propaganda branches of all those who are involved in this vast educational conspiracy are forced to work harder and harder. The time-table for the great restructuring (the new paradigm) must then be advanced. Too many people are catching on that the real goal of the new educational paradigm is actually governmental control. The home school movement is a response to that discovery. I fear, however, that when propaganda is no longer effective, other means will be found (judicial means) to mandate their program. Meanwhile, the voucher system (which in truth is an example of the functioning of a truly democratic society) must be opposed with all the considerable resources at the disposal of those who have the most to lose from its implementation. It is truly a key issue for our times. It is an issue on which Americans need to be informed and to seek God.

In March 1993, the federal government introduced its educational wish list, calling it Goals 2000. It had been several years in preparation, but its time had finally come. Most Americans are indeed alarmed about the sad state of education in our nation and are therefore hopeful that the federal government might find the key to improve the educational situation. The goals mentioned in the Excellence in Education Act will prove that the federal government is unable to actually change the educational situation in America, except perhaps to make it worse. It will prove that it is easy for government to promulgate edicts and to mandate change without actually being able to do anything of substance to implement their wish list. It will also prove that they never had any intention of implementing their grandiose goals. It is all window-dressing to disguise their real intention: a giant power grab.

Although foolishness is perhaps potentially infinite, we can measure a megaquantum leap in absurdity between terrible ideas like whole language approach and the open classroom/open school idea. There is a quantum leap between those polished gems of absurdity and the bedrock of OBE. I can already tell you what the outcome of Outcome-Based Education will be: skyrocketing costs, plummeting academic achievement, loss of local control of education, and an educational system which would have been John Dewey's delight.

18

Feminism and Abortion

"Human life must be respected and protected absolutely from the moment of conception. From the first moment of his existence, a person must be recognized as having the rights of a person—among which is the inviolable right of every innocent being to life." (*Catechism of the Catholic Church*).

There is no more divisive issue in American society today than the abortion question. Unrestricted abortion on demand (one of the fondest dreams of New Age secular humanists) is being driven largely by the politically correct group. At the core of this group and at the core of this issue is one of the meanest, most fragmenting groups in America: gender feminists.

I think it is important to define terms. There are primarily two types of feminists—equity feminists and gender feminists. Those who support equity feminism believe that women should have the same opportunities that men have. They insist on equality before the law and equal pay for equal work, in social justice and fair play. In many ways, equity feminism is a celebration of women which is based upon logic and upon the ideal of feminine worth and dignity which is promoted and taught by the Christian Scriptures. At its best, equity feminism is an excellent and worthy cause. Its greatest danger, of course, is that in an immoral society it will seek to guarantee women the same rights to sin that men have, rights "won" during the sexual revolution of the 1960s. When and where that happens, a good idea goes terribly wrong. The simple truth is that without the moral compass of godly absolutes, even the best of human ideas will wander off course. Most movements and people go wrong a degree at a time. Given enough time, however, the degrees mount up, and people and movements end up far from their original destination.

In many ways, true gender feminists have little in common with true equity feminists. Gender feminists reject both facts and logic. In their more extreme form they do embrace homosexuality, witchcraft, goddess worship, and a paganized type of Christianity. They are outspoken foes of the traditional family and see men as their natural enemies. They are also a major force behind the great increase in the number of divorces in America over the past few decades.

The true essence of feminism (just as it is for witchcraft) is the pursuit of power. Gender feminism has a three-pronged agenda. The first is to destroy all male domination (real and imagined) in order to establish female domination. William F. Buckley wrote that the radical feminist movement "offers a prescription for radical change that is as simple as it is drastic; reject whatever is tainted with patriarchy and replace it with something embodying gynecentric values."[1] Their second "cause celebre" is the redefinition of the concept of family and the promotion of homosexuality. The third is to insure that American women have the option of uncontested, unlimited, taxpayer supported abortion on demand. Gender feminists currently have a strong and growing influence in American colleges and universities, often ruling through intimidation. Their course offerings have little to do with academics, but a lot to do with the feminist agenda. They also have made significant inroads in the American judiciary and media.

Since our Supreme Court made abortion on demand national policy in 1973, a baby has been murdered every three minutes in America, producing a type of holocaust that dwarfs Hitler's Holocaust. There are, of course, some striking similarities. The word *holocaust* was derived from a fifth century Greek word which referred to the Jewish temple burnt offering, a religious sacrifice made to Jehovah. Hitler's Holocaust was a type of fiery burnt offering made by Hitler and the Nazis as they offered up Jews and Christians as an offering to Satan. Hitler's sacrifice, based upon his demonic and occult world view was a type of pagan religious sacrifice, a sacrifice which took modern Germany back to its pagan, barbaric, and Satanic prehistoric roots. The sacrifice of innocent children in the name of a "right to privacy" is also a religious sacrifice. It is a sacrifice of human life to the god of selfishness, Satan. It is a modern return to the abomination which God judged in ancient Israel—the offering of its children to the cruel pagan deity Moloch. Those sons and daughters of Israel were burned alive in the arms or stomachs of brazen idols in order to gain the favor of their demonic deity. American children are dismembered or burned alive in the womb by saline solutions. Technology has improved, but man's heart has not. In the supreme irony of our age, we seek to protect and preserve bald eagles, whales, seals, spotted owls and timber wolves, but we throw away our children.

The country was stunned and outraged when Susan Smith killed her own children. When the ever-present television reporters canvassed her hometown for a reaction, one young woman declared that "any mother who murders her own children deserves to die." In the light of the abortion question, her response was highly ironic. The sad truth is that infanticide is the philosophy that is behind abortion carried to the next level.

It is important for Americans to realize three very important things. Our nationwide policy of abortion-on-demand was neither voted for by our people nor enacted by our legislators. It was simply what Supreme Court Justice Byron White called "an act of raw judicial power." William Quirk made the point that America has fallen under the despotism of judicial tyranny. Our courts see themselves in the role of advancing the secular humanist agenda in society. "In our current setting, it has become unfortunately quite common for the courts to attempt to legislate their own social plans from the bench, overriding democratically-elected legislatures and creating 'constitutional rights' which did not formerly exist."[2]

The second thing people must realize is that mankind is not capable of attaining true justice apart from God. Most people have already realized the third point; the Supreme Court is not infallible; that just because something is "legal" in a specific time and place, it is not necessarily moral. As an illustration of this point, I offer two proofs. In his autobiography *Mein Kampf*, Adolf Hitler announced his plan to "deal with the Jewish problem." It was a position to which he resolutely held throughout the war, constantly expanding its scope and fullest possible implementation. The Holocaust was the result of Hitler's zeal for the mass murder of Jews and Christians. The Holocaust, however, was built upon the rulings of German courts (which obediently did the bidding of Hitler). When the Germans voted as a nation for Hitler to become a sort of "living constitution" in Germany, they blindly and trustingly gave Hitler the right to rule by executive order. When some Germans began to complain about the mistreatment of Jews, Hitler had them "legally" redefined successively as "non-citizens," "non-Germans," and finally "non-human." Thus deprived of all legal protection, the Jews were sent "legally" to their deaths. The Nazi state took upon itself the right to "legally" decide who should live and who should die in Germany. Hitler practiced on Germans beginning in the euthanasia campaign of 1939. It was a program designed to purify Germany of those who did not have lives worthy of being lived. The Nazis purified Germany of as many as 275,000 of their fellow Germans before they fixed their attention more fully on the Jews. The sad fact is that Hitler used democracy to "legally" overthrow democracy in Germany.

The American Supreme Court, which has redefined itself, now seems almost all-powerful in secular America. It is clearly not infallible. The *Roe vs. Wade* ruling is an excellent example of this. In many ways it is similar to the *Dred Scott* decision of 1857. In this ruling (for those of you who are a bit weak in American history, including most Americans who have graduated from public schools in the past twenty-five years), the Supreme Court ruled that blacks were not actually American citizens. They were thus deprived of the protection of the law and of their civil rights under the law. The *Dred Scott* decision was an effort to come to a political compromise on the question of slavery which was dividing society. In the end, however, no compromise was possible, and the Civil War was fought to solve what Abraham Lincoln called "a moral, a social, and a political wrong." The *Roe vs. Wade* decision is also a morally, socially, and politically wrong decision. It is a "defiance of the long-held Western ethic of intrinsic and equal value for every human life regardless of its stage, condition, or status."[3]

The abortion issue is a perfect illustration of Charles Colson's belief that "today's Western culture rejects absolutes and enshrines only self-indulgence."[4] Solzhenitsyn said, "It is time, in the West, to defend not so much human rights as human obligations."[5] The steady diet of selfishness and self-indulgence stultifies the soul and slowly deadens the spirit. Mother Theresa, who lamented this individual and corporate poverty of spirit warned, "Abortion is a crime that kills not only the child but the consciences of all involved."[6] "What a strange irony it is that the Liberal Mind today is for Herod and the slaughter of the innocents in preference to Mother Theresa's readiness to take in and care for any unwanted baby?"[7]

Predictably, we are seeing a preoccupation with death reminiscent of the immoral/amoral conduct in the pre-Nazi Weimar republic. This society not only condoned and promoted immorality, it endorsed a type of Hegelian social reasoning. "Practicality and utility" replaced moral, religious, and ethical values. Abortion and euthanasia joined hands in German society to guide the nation toward an acceptance of Hitler and the Holocaust. A moral vacuum always leads to a debasement of human life. Deception leads to destruction. The Nuremberg war trials illustrated how momentous events came from small beginnings. In Germany, it started with the acceptance of the idea that there are lives that are not worthy of being lived. America seems to be following the path that Nazi Germany took in its selfish and callous disregard for human life. The principle of the sanctity of human life is being sacrificed on the altar of the sovereign self. A nation that murders its own children and elderly is capable of anything.

History taught the world in World War II that evil cannot be appeased. It must be opposed. History also taught us that the church in Germany did too little, too late.

After a speech, pro-life activist Penny Lea was approached by an old man. Weeping, he told her the following story.

I lived in Germany during the Nazi holocaust. I considered myself a Christian. I attended church since I was a small boy. We had heard the stories of what was happening to the Jews, but like most people today in the country, we tried to distance ourselves from the reality of what was really taking place. What could anyone do to stop it?

A railroad track ran behind our small church, and each Sunday morning we would hear the whistle from the distance and then the clacking of wheels moving over the track. We became disturbed when one Sunday we noticed cries coming from the train as it passed by. We grimly realized that the train was carrying Jews. They were like cattle in those cars!

Week after week that train whistle would blow. We would dread to hear the sound of those wheels because we knew that the Jews would begin to cry out to us as they passed our church. It was so terribly disturbing! We could do nothing to help those poor miserable people, yet their screams tormented us. We knew exactly at what time the whistle would blow, and we decided that the only way to keep from being so disturbed by their cries was to start singing our hymns. By the time that the train came rumbling past the churchyard, we were singing at the top of our voices. If some of the screams reached our ears, we'd sing a little louder until we could hear them no more. Years have passed and no one talks about it much anymore, but I still hear that train whistle in my sleep. I can still hear them crying out for help. God forgive all of us who called ourselves Christians, yet did nothing to intervene.[8]

The church in America must not make the same mistake. God has made the Church to be the pillar and support of truth in society. He has made the Church to fill the role of the conscience of society. Of course, it is also true that throughout history, those who spoke God's truth in society were often punished and killed for speaking it. The Dutch theologian, Abraham Kuyper, advised the Church to forsake the pursuit of peace and to take a righteous stand, to "lay bare our convictions before friend and enemy, with all the fire of our faith." The Apostle Paul gave us all a starting point. In 2 Corinthians 10:13 he wrote that we all have a sphere of interest. That sphere may be very small or it may be very large. It begins, however, exactly where we are. It begins with prayer. Within that sphere of interest, we offer ourselves to God, trusting that He will enable us to have an impact for Him, trusting Him that it is "Not by might, nor by power, but by His Spirit" (Zech. 4:6) that we will serve. Our service must remain squarely and solidly within the biblical parameters of our rela- tionship with God. Within the parameters the ends never justify the means, for God weighs both motives and methods. Those who stand for the prolife posi- tion, for example, cannot use the same methods as those who support the prodeath position. David Thibodaux expressed it perfectly when he said,

> I think that we should also be quick to point out that anyone who bombs an abortion clinic or shoots a doctor who performs abortions be- comes guilty not only of a heinous act that sim- ply cannot be condoned but also of the same hypocrisy that is so characteristic of the politi- cally correct phenomenon. In other words, one cannot kill in the cause of "right to life."[9]

The liberal humanist media makes use of every such opportunity to malign the entire prolife move- ment.

The Church must play the role in society that God has given it to play; the role of being salt and light.

19

The Brand New, Same Old New Age Movement

I hadn't communicated with my favorite cousin for thirty years. She and I had been close all throughout school. We went to the same grade school, same junior high school, and finally graduated from high school together. We lost touch with each other after graduation. Just for fun, I decided to write her a letter one day. Eventually she called me and we chatted, catching up on the courses our lives had taken. After a bit, I told her that I had written a book on the New Age movement. Although she is a bright woman, a successful career woman, she had never heard of the New Age movement. I sometimes forget that many people have somehow missed that bit of news. I dedicate this chapter to all those who, like my own dear cousin, have never heard of the New Age movement and who have thus probably never considered the true implications of the bottom line of the New Age movement: the New World Order. It is my firm belief that a proper understanding of the source and substance of the New Age movement is essential for those who wish to understand the present political and spiritual climate in America.

We are now living in a period of history which could be summed up by a line written by Charles Dickens as "the best of times and the worst of times." It is the best of times for those who are waiting for the imminent return of their Lord Jesus Christ. It is a prophetic time when the Church will play perhaps its most significant role in human history—a time of high adventure. The Church is called to be faithful and joyful in a period of time when many will be fearful, fickle, confused and discouraged. It will be the worst of times for those whose hope is in man and in man's problem-solving abilities. The prophet Jeremiah said that those who trust in man are cursed. This decade will prove that to be true.

We are quickly moving toward the end of this millennium. We are moving toward a new age in human history—an age which has been predicted by occultists and soothsayers of all varieties as well as prophetically by students of Bible prophecy. Both groups are in agreement that there will indeed be a new age. They are not in agreement on how this new age will come, the goals of this new age, who will be in charge of the program, and on its eventual outcome.

I believe that the Bible speaks of the current New Age movement as the great spiritual deception that will bring this age to a close. It is a movement which is based on the terminal and definitive merging of the humanistic and the demonic, a movement of deception and lawlessness which is based upon an appeal to human pride. The final result of the New Age movement will be the introduction of the New World Order, whose true face can be seen in Psalm 2. In this Psalm, rebellious mankind (both Gentile and Jewish) conspires to throw off the rulership of a holy God in order to go into business for itself. The result of this conspiracy can be seen in the Book of Revelation.

The bottom line of the New Age movement is that it is a rejection of God the Father, of Christ Jesus, of true biblical Christianity, and of the Bible. It is a movement, composed of both the deceivers and the deceived, which hopes to rebuild the spiritual system that was represented by the Tower of Babel, an ancient merging of the humanistic and the demonic, the seat of all false religions.

The modern New Age movement can be traced back to pre-World War I Germany. Germany had been specifically prepared by the antichrist spirit. It was a land which had rejected God's Word but which had enthusiastically embraced occultism, humanism, Darwinism (with which it was especially fascinated), and anti-Semitism. Germany was sort of a spiritual test case, a spiritual microcosm, an indicator of what was to come. The genius of the New Age movement has been that chameleon-like, it has been able to seem to be all things to all people as it has relentlessly pursued its program, working almost invisibly in society like an evil leaven. Although the New Age movement now boasts tens of thousands of entry points into its program, many people remain virtually unaware of its presence, its plan, its scope, and its power. The New Age movement (which is an umbrella term), and which went primetime and mainstream in the 1970s, has largely become invisible by becoming ultravisible in the 1990s. By a constant process of the reeducation of society, it has become more and more accepted. (T. S. Eliot said that "paganism has all the most valuable advertising space." That is certainly true.)

Although almost everyone has become aware of the term "New Age movement," I have found that very few people (Christians included) are able to explain it or define it (including people who are clearly New Agers). Once people mention their impressions on Shirley MacLaine, crystals, mantras, New Age music,

the Harmonic Convergence, and some assorted Eastern mystics and gurus, they are generally at a loss to go
much further. I readily admit that this particular short
list does not seem to pose much of a threat to civilization. It also does not truly represent the essence and
substance of the New Age movement. It is unfortunately much wider and deeper than those superficial
concepts and personalities. The New Age movement is
so sinister because it is in a sense the summing up of
all the other spiritual movements of evil in history. I
believe it to be, therefore, the culmination of Satan's
plan for mankind. It is a movement of singular importance because it is designed to be the terminal spiritual
movement in world history, the Satanic vehicle that is
designed to sweep mankind into the Satanic New World
Order, into a grand and glorious new era, into its own
version of a secular yet spiritual millennium.

The New Age movement is based on a web of
Satanic lies, whose true essence is deception and destruction. In truth it is more of a societal mindset than
it is a true movement. The term *movement* suggests a
tangible, coherent and clearly apparent leadership and
goals. The human leader of the New Age movement
has not yet appeared, but he has been chosen. The
true guiding power of the New Age movement is invisible to the undiscerning eye because it is a spiritual
power. This spiritual power is able to deceive and
manipulate people toward its own spiritual and political ends. Like nazism, the New Age movement is a
spiritual system which can be translated into a political
reality. Those who are being manipulated are often
simply following their own special interests and agendas within the larger movement. They are usually not
even aware that they are being woven into the fabric of
a larger spiritual tapestry, being used to implement a
larger spiritual program.

The New Age movement is a spiritual beast system, a forerunner of the beast system which emerges in the Book of Revelation. The beast system is nothing less than the kingdom of the Antichrist. It is rather like the hydra of Greek mythology. The hydra was an evil serpent with nine heads. When one of the heads was cut off, two new ones grew in its place. In our modern vernacular, the hydra stands for "any persistent or ever-increasing evil with many sources and causes." The many heads represent the many aspects of the New Age movement. The surface appearance may therefore be confusing to many people, for the movement itself cannot be easily understood by analyzing the heads. The heads do not necessarily suggest a consistent comprehensive spiritual pattern. It can only be understood by looking at the twin roots which empower and sustain the proliferating heads. The twin roots of the New Age movement are of humanism and demonism, both revolts against the God of the Bible. The goal of the system itself, however, is to facilitate the emergence of the worldwide beast kingdom which will be under the rulership of the Antichrist, a satanically possessed human being who will rule over this spiritual-political empire.

Billy Graham believes that the white horse in the sixth chapter of the Book of the Revelation symbolizes "counterfeit religion, with secular, anti-God, and anti-Christian belief systems." I think that the white horse rider is the Antichrist, going forth to conquer. His appearance suggests a worldwide system of deception, a system of false religions. Its defining characteristics will be a toleration for any type of deception and a militant hostility toward both Christianity and Judaism (Matt. 24:9-12). It will be a system that encompasses both humanistic and the demonic religions, a prophetic indicator of all that is to come. The rider on the white horse symbolizes the spiritual leadership which will orchestrate a period of profound spiritual deception throughout the earth. The deceiving white horse rider will precipitate the arrival of the three apocalyptic horses and riders which follow him, riders who will unleash dreadful suffering upon the entire planet. Peace will disappear from the planet. The whole earth will be one vast Sarajevo. Deception will have led to destruction. I believe that the false system symbolized by the white horse is that of the New Age movement.

The New Age movement is not an end in itself. It is the means to an end. It is the final rejection of the authority of God and the exaltation of humanistic pride and demonic power, a final merging of humanism and demonism into a final worldwide system. Demonism is, of course, nothing other than satanism. Demons knowingly serve Satan and use deception or temptation to enlist the aid of mankind in their service of Satan and in the implementation of his program upon the earth. Hell was not created for man, but as a punishment for Satan and his demons. Fallen mankind "inherited" hell by throwing its lot in with Satan. By associating itself with him, it inherited his fate.

The dandelion is a sturdy and prolific plant. As anyone who has a yard knows, if you clip the dandelion down to the ground it is soon back again, intent on the business of producing thousands of dandelion seeds which travel near and far on the smallest of breezes. The only way to deal with the dandelion, the only way to stop it from reproducing, is to deal with the roots. That is equally true in a spiritual sense in the lives of people. A movement is rather like a whole field of dandelions, for movements are made up of individuals. Individuals must be reached one at a time with the truth.

John 16:8 describes the role of the Holy Spirit in the world. The Holy Spirit convicts the world of sin, righteousness, and judgment. He convicts the world of sin, not of "sins." Sins come from the root of sin. The sin from which other sins draw their strength and source is the rejection of Christ Jesus. The rejection of the biblical Christ Jesus is the fruit of the working of the antichrist spirit. This spirit works to cause people to reject truth, sowing deception and reaping destruction. God's truth destroys error and His life and light prevail over darkness and death. John 17:3 instructs us that eternal life is not simply living forever. It is the foundation of a relationship with God the Father through Jesus the Son by a revelation of the Holy Spirit. God's truth (if it is believed and acted upon) destroys the twin roots of humanism and demonism (which are both rebellions against God), the tap roots of the New Age movement. A person who is rooted in humanism or demonism produces fruit that is according to his roots. Those who are born again through the ministry of God's Word by the Holy Spirit are rooted and grounded in the love of God. The fruit they produce brings glory to God.

Our nation is at a great fork in the road. Crucial decisions determine the direction our nation will take spiritually, historically, and culturally. We are perhaps at a cultural version of what Scripture teaches will happen during the Millennial Kingdom of Christ—the dividing of the goats and the sheep. The goats are directed into judgment. The sheep are directed into the tender bosom of God's love. The determination of directions is made by God, but He simply enforces in an eternal sense the choices that both groups had already made. The ultimate and eternal separation from God is prefigured by the choices that men and women make here and now. Truth is not an academic question. It is a matter of life and death.

The choices are becoming ever more clear. The road separates at Romans 1:21-22—a knowing rejection of God's truth or a voluntary submission to God's truth. The battle lines are drawn.

Make no mistake. We as Bible-believing evangelical Christians are locked in a battle. This is
not a friendly gentleman's discussion. It is a life
and death conflict between the spiritual hosts
of wickedness and those who claim the name of
Christ. It is a conflict on the level of ideas between two fundamentally opposed views of truth
and reality. It is a conflict on the level of actions
between a complete moral perversion and chaos
and God's absolutes.[1]

20

Satan's Favorite Lie: Evolution

Satan is by nature a liar. He is good at what he does because he has had a lot of practice. Satan's most effective lies appeal to the human weak spot: the ego. Satan gives people a choice that they might prefer to God's stated opinion, His Word. That tactic worked well in the Garden of Eden, and it has been working well ever since. Satan's favorite lie for modern man is the lie of evolution. It is an ancient lie which has been repackaged for maximum effect in the modern secular humanist world. The theory of evolution has always had a strong appeal to man's pride. Although Darwin popularized it in 1859, the ancient Egyptians, Sumerians, and Babylonians believed in it wholeheartedly. It was a key part of their occult belief system.

Chapter 2 of the book of 2 Thessalonians describes the state of society at the end of the age. Paul wrote this letter to reassure the Thessalonian church that they had not missed the Rapture of the Church. He first established a framework for them by explaining that there must first be a great apostasy in the Church, a great falling away from the faith. That description did not fit their age, but it surely does fit our age. This apostasy will lead to the full and final appearance of the Antichrist, an appearance which is now being restrained by the Holy Spirit. This satanically possessed human vessel will eventually make and break a covenant with Israel, finally proclaiming himself as divine in the newly built temple in Jerusalem. This will also precipitate a wave of worldwide anti-Semitism as well as a worldwide revival as 144,000 sealed Jews (12,000 from each tribe) spread throughout the world, preaching God's Word. They will minister God's light in a time of worldwide darkness. Those who heed the message, turning from darkness to light will be saved. Those who have a love for the truth will respond to God's truth, and they will share that truth with others, shaking with their truth the societal structure of lies which Satan has so carefully and thoroughly fabricated. One of those lies will be the lie of evolution. I believe that society has been conditioned for a long time toward the appearance of the Antichrist. The Antichrist will burst upon the world scene, portraying himself as the definitive example of a "perfectly evolved man," the prototype of a new species of man which the New Agers call Homo Noeticus. His message to mankind will be that under his leadership, mankind will develop the spark of humanity which is supposed to be within each person, fanning this spark into a full-fledged leap into divinity under his leadership. Backed by politically and financially powerful supporters, this satanically possessed man will also draw tremendous spiritual support from those who are impressed by his ability to perform spiritual signs and wonders. He will portray himself as the one who has come to fulfill the ethic of all the religions of the world.

The theory of evolution has always appealed strongly to the pride of mankind. The theory of evolution has itself evolved over the years. Even Darwin, who said "We may suppose" over eight hundred times in his two primary works on evolution (a lot of supposing for a supposedly scientific treatise) would be amazed at the evolutionary beliefs of modern Darwinists. They have truly gone from the ridiculous to the sublimely ridiculous. In the 1950s, the apostate priest Teilhard de Chardin came up with the idea of the Omega point, a theory somewhat akin to Carl Jung's idea of mass consciousness. Teilhard believed that the corporate spiritual evolution of the human race will create a type of mass consciousness, an overmind into which all mankind will be able to tap. In the 1970s the Russians came up with the idea of "punctuated equilibrium," a theory which teaches that one species can change suddenly and spontaneously into another. The New Agers then topped that theory with "transformational evolution." In this cosmic plan, mankind (just as the animals did) will be able to take a sudden, quantum leap into godhood. Frank Peretti humorously summed up this absurd proposition by saying, "Everybody gets to be God except Jesus." The truth concerning evolution is simple. It is a lie. It is in fact such a preposterous and absurd theory that it takes far more faith to believe in it than it does to believe in creationism. In his book, *The Collapse of Evolution*, Scott M. Huse gives this amusing little poem to describe the leap of faith required to believe in evolution: "As I was sitting in my chair, I knew it had no bottom there, nor legs, or back, but I just sat Ignoring little things like that."[1]

A belief in evolution enables mankind to reject the demands and requirements of a holy God. This desire to live as an autonomous being, a being independent of God is the primary reason that people choose to believe in evolution. They fear the implications of the alternative: creationism. Honest scientists have long admitted that the theory of evolution simply does not hold together. It has been flawed from the beginning. Despite all the frantic and fruitless scientific searches done in the last 130 years, science has not been able to come up with one example of one species turning into another species. This was, of course, Darwin's major speculative "scientific" revelation. The truth is simple. Secular humanists like the theory of evolution because it eliminates their responsibility and accountability toward God.

The theory of evolution has affected the wide spectrum of American thought. The theory of evolution has long held a monopoly in American public schools and in colleges and universities where it is taught as unquestioned truth. Evolution has likewise been taught as truth by the electronic media. In recent years, evolution has been adopted as truth by the field of psychology. The ultrahumanistic, me-centered "pop psychology" sees great possibilities for self-improvement and self-perfection in the theory of evolution. Psychology embraces the idea that man is born good (rejecting the biblical position of Original Sin) and is actually infinitely perfectible. (God is on record in Genesis 8:21 as voicing the opinion that "The intent of man's heart is evil from his youth." I guess poor God has a lot to learn from the psychological point of view.) The English humorist G. K. Chesterton wrote that Original Sin is the one biblical doctrine which can be empirically proven over thirty-five hundred years of recorded history.

"Christians have come to realize that the theory of evolution has much greater implications for society than merely what students will be taught about the origination of the planets, stars, and species."[2] Scott M. Huse writes that "What a person believes about his or her origin will condition that person's lifestyle and affect his or her ultimate destiny." He believes that

our current social and moral problems are
largely a result of the humanistic philosophy
which has been spawned by evolutionary thinking. The so-called "new morality" we are presently witnessing is actually "no morality," the
inevitable result of the atheistic, evolutionary
philosophy. Indeed, there are virtually no areas
of thought and life today which have remained
impervious to the effects of this popular viewpoint.[3]

It has long been my belief that Nazi Germany was
a type of microcosm which will eventually be experienced as a worldwide macrocosm during the Great
Tribulation. The part played in Germany by Hitler will
be fulfilled worldwide by the Antichrist. It is also my
belief that some of the key "philosophies of man" which
enabled Hitler to come to power in Germany are firmly
in place in our own society. Since I have written of
these beliefs at length in two other books, I will confine myself here to the part evolution played in facili-
tating Hitler's rise to power.

It was neither accidental nor incidental that Germany so enthusiastically received as truth the theories
of Darwin. Germany had been seized by a type of
nationalism which was based in part upon its return to
paganism, its profound anti-Semitism, and its belief in
Aryan superiority and a worldwide Aryan destiny. Evolution gave to those who were so willingly self-deceived
the "scientific validation" of their racial theories. They
believed that German Aryans and Germany itself were
evolving into a caste of spiritual, military, and political
overlords.

Darwin's first book was published in 1859. It entered into the German consciousness around the same
time that German seminaries were rejecting the validity and authority of God's Word. Darwinism flourished
in Germany like an unchecked bacterial infection be-

tween 1860 and its first major intrusion into American society—the Scopes monkey trial in 1925. The evil fruit of Darwinism in Germany produced an evil harvest by the beginning of World War I. The same crop of deception would not mature in America for another generation.

Hitler built a political state partially on his own concept of social Darwinism, on the survival of the fittest. Of course, once Hitler was in power, he decided who was fit to live. Darwinism was a key foundational concept in Hitler's racist edifice, and it ultimately provided him a justification for genocide. Hitler resolved to speed up the evolutionary process by spiritual development, eugenics, and the technology of death. For Hitler, the technology of death included the process of war and of extermination. They were his ways of speeding up the process of natural selection. In the process, Hitler caused Germany to become a country which was preoccupied with death. The same preoccupation is occurring in America today. Human life is progressively being treated as insignificant. The Supreme Court has given American parents the right to sentence millions of American children to death in the name of a right to privacy—a right which is surely nowhere in the Constitution. Once a national conscience is debased and destroyed, nearly anything is possible for a selfish populace. It might be euthanasia. It might be infanticide. It might be concentration camps, reeducation centers for the evolutionarily challenged.

21

God's New Plan:
The Real New Man

Satan always establishes his false plan according to the revelation of God's true plan. The goal of counterfeiting is to substitute things that are false for things that are true and to have what is false accepted as being true. The work of the antichrist spirit is to oppose, deny, or pervert the truth. The most effective type of deception is always self-deception since people are always most likely to be led astray at the point where they most want to be led astray. Humanistic mankind, for example, is most easily led astray at the crossroad where human pride is confronted with God's truth. Since he cannot travel both roads, man must make a choice. At that juncture, Satan proposes alternative truths, truths designed to be more acceptable to the human ego. It is incredible how prideful mankind bends over backward to believe Satanic falsehood promoted as truth simply because it appeals to his ego. Pride does go before a fall. Satan should know, for he is the prototype for that particular experience. The ideas of evolution and reincarnation are Satanic alternatives to God's truth. These ideas may be absurd, but they are attractive to many people in our society, simply because mankind loves to believe that he is in control of his own destiny. (In a recent survey, a group of people who specifically identified themselves as Christians were asked by what criterion they believed themselves to be Christian. Eighty-one percent of them said that it was simply that they believed themselves to be. In other words, it is perfectly acceptable to be a Christian on one's own terms—even if they are not God's terms.) God's truth and God's plan cannot be rejected with impunity. There will always be a price to pay. In the long run, only His truth will prevail.

The spiritual bottom line of the New Age movement is to produce a perfect man, a planetary citizen in a New World Order. In this, the New Age movement is the spiritual heir of nazism, which also hoped to produce an Aryan god-man who would rule in Hitler's New Order. Mankind's hope to produce the perfect man through managed evolution is not possible simply because it is based upon a lie. God, however, does have a plan to produce a perfect new man. His plan will succeed. His plan, in fact, has already succeeded. God's plan has existed since before the foundation of the world. All human history flows between the points already established by God in eternity past and eternity future. Since God sees the end from the beginning (and vice-versa), that makes God the ultimate historian. His viewpoint alone is perfectly accurate. Those points are Alpha and Omega. There is nothing before them and nothing after them. Alpha and Omega refer to Jesus Christ, the source and the goal of history. All of God's plan is summed up in Him (Eph. 1:10). All human history will likewise be summed up in Him in one way or another—either in redemption or in judgment. Jesus Christ is the cornerstone of God's plan. He is either a stepping-stone into the family of God or a stumbling block for those who reject Him. For those who accept Christ, He is the foundation stone for a relationship with the Father. For those who reject Him, Jesus is a stone of judgment which will crush those who have exalted themselves against Him.

All of those who are building upon the sure foundation of Christ Jesus are called living stones. They are being built together into a living temple through which praises to God are being offered. The individual believers are living stones, each in right relationship to Christ Himself and also to the other believers. Together they form a temple of praise, a building which is beautiful, not because of stained glass or majestic organs, but because it manifests the grace of God and the beautiful character of Christ. This holy temple will be removed from the earth intact at the moment of the Rapture of the Church. This holy temple, constructed of living stones, is the corporate new man of God's plan. The new man is a corporate revelation of Christ made up of all the individual believers on the face of the earth.

God the Father has ordained that this body of believers will belong to His Son, Christ Jesus. They have been created by Him through His Spirit to be the eternal companion of His Son. The Book of Ephesians speaks of this as a mystery, something which man can understand only as God reveals it to him. God's mystery is revealed in His Word by His Spirit. This eternal companion is revealed in Ephesians in various illustrative manifestations, all of which reveal an identification with Christ Jesus. The eternal companion of Christ is represented as His body on earth, as His temple, as a godly mystery, as a new man, as His bride, and as a loyal soldier. The brave soldier of Ephesians chapter six is standing fast on the ground which has been won by Christ, awaiting the moment when he will be raptured to be forever with His Lord. Each of the identities of the believer in the Book of Ephesians is a corporate identity.

A lot of good plans come to naught. The life of modern man without God can be summed up by Schubert's "Unfinished Symphony." Somehow, all of man's great and glorious potential and plans always fall short. Since God is perfect, His plan is also perfect. God's perfect plan will therefore come to perfect fruition. In Matthew 5:48, Jesus said, "Therefore you are to be perfect, as your heavenly Father is perfect." It is both a command and an invitation. There are stages in the perfection which our salvation in Christ brings. The perfect work of Christ Jesus has given us positional perfection. God sees us in Christ as citizens of heaven. It is a legally completed transaction. Christians have been sealed by the Holy Spirit as a proof of the completion of the transaction, as a proof of His ownership of us, and as a proof of the coming glory that will be ours. When we stand in the presence of God, we shall be truly perfect. That is ultimate perfection. As long as we are on this earth, however, we continue to be perfected daily by the Holy Spirit into the image of Jesus Christ. On this earth, we are called to be mature, fully grown, and fully equipped, but not perfect in the heavenly sense of the term. The Lord is returning for a mature church, a church which is perfectly identified with Him and perfectly committed to Him. This is the mystery that God is now revealing to the world.

God's plan for the redemption of mankind predates the creation of Adam and Eve. Since God's foreknowledge is perfect, He knew that Adam and Eve would be seduced. Adam was a good plan, but not a perfect plan. The failure of that plan was due to the inherent weakness of man. Man is a limited being. It is also illustrative of the fact that man does not have it in himself to follow God perfectly; neither the will nor the ability. Jesus was God's perfect plan. Adam demonstrated that man needs a saviour. Jesus Christ is that saviour. Adam was created. Those who are born again are recreated in righteousness and holiness (Eph. 5:24) by the Holy Spirit. God does not repair hearts. He gives people new hearts, hearts open to Him. They are born again through God's Spirit, severing forever their relationship to Adam and all that he represents by establishing a relationship with God through Christ that will last for all eternity. When He adopts us as children into His family, our hearts respond by crying "Abba," Father! Our spirits become alive to Him and conscious of the awfulness of sin. Desiring to please a holy Father, we begin to walk as beloved children. We learn to walk as Jesus walked—in love (Eph. 5:2), as children of light (Eph. 5:8), and in wisdom (Eph. 5:15). We walk in the newness of life that one would expect to find in a new creation.

The new man, the body of Christ, is God's most amazing creation—His Church.

God has a threefold redemptive plan. It is a plan which defines clearly the future of the Church, the Jews, and the nations of the world (the Gentile world community). God's plan has always centered upon Christ. It still does. Epistemology is the study of the theory, the origin, the nature, and the limits of human knowledge. Although human knowledge has limits, God's knowledge is unlimited. It is therefore worthwhile and beneficial to appeal to God when we reach one of the limits of human knowledge. God's response is revelation. It is humbling for mankind to realize that we can only go so far on our own. It is also exciting to know that God is willing to share His revelation with those who are truly willing to receive it. He has freely shared His redemptive plan with mankind, and those who have eyes to see will see it. Satan also has a threefold plan. His plan is not redemptive in nature. It is solely destructive. It runs parallel to God's threefold plan, also dealing with the Church, the Jews, and the nations.

Satan's plan for the Church is to slander, corrupt, and oppose it. He knows that his time is short. The Rapture of the Church will mark the end of the Church age, which began at Pentecost. It will also mark the beginning of Satan's confinement to planet earth, the beginning of the Great Tribulation period, which is so powerfully depicted in the Book of Revelation. It will also number the days that will lead to his permanent defeat.

Satan's plan for the Jews is to deceive them into worshipping him. Once that plan fails, it will be his goal to destroy every living Jew in a worldwide holocaust.

Satan's plan for the Gentile world community is to corrupt and pervert it, conforming it to his own image, preparing it for the emergence of the Antichrist and his own brief reign of terror in a worldwide Societas Satanas.

Time is short. We are living at the end of what the Bible calls the mystery age. The mystery age began with the rejection of their messiah by the Jews and the subsequent birth of the Church at Pentecost. The Church will soon be raptured, returning to earth with her Lord at the end of the Great Tribulation, at the beginning of the millennium. The mystery age will end with the nation of Israel receiving Christ Jesus as her Messiah in national humility and with repentance toward the end of the tribulation period, and with preaching the gospel throughout the Gentile world. The eyes of the whole world have been fixed on Israel since 1948. The return of the Jews to their ancient homeland is a dramatic prophetic sign that God's redemptive plan in Christ is focused specifically upon Israel like a laser beam. All that remains is for God to start the prophetic time clock on its final circuit.

22

A Final Word

Much of this book is about truth. It is about the truth of John 10:10, that Satan's mission is to kill, steal, and to destroy. It is also about the other half of John 10:10, that Jesus came to give us a way out of that process. The way out, however, involves making a choice. It involves responding to the truth. It is only truth applied that sets people free. It is about John 8:31-32, that the disciples of Christ will abide in His Word. It is about Ezra 7:10, that the commission of a godly person is to know, to live, and to teach God's Word. Ezra 7:10 is a ministry of salt and light in a society which is more and more in love with sin and darkness. It is a society which is described in Romans 1:18-32 as a sinful and reprobate society which exchanged the truth of God for a lie and which exchanged the glory of God for the pursuit of idolatry. Francis Schaeffer has called this a "post-Christian age." By definition, that would mean that this is an age of idolatry. In some ways, the Church has come full circle (although the world has remained in the same place). The Church was born in a time of cruel idolatry in order to faithfully preach and live the gospel of truth—

a gospel whose core is the testimony of Jesus Christ. It is this gospel which divides. There is, in fact, no sanctification without separation. It is this holy separation which sent John to the island of Patmos as a man who was deemed to be politically incorrect. It is this gospel which gave us the prophetic Book of Revelation. (It is Revelation, not Revelations, because the book is a revelation of Jesus Christ.) It is the message in Revelation 12:11 that amplifies the truth in John 8:31-32, focusing it like a laser beam into the hearts and the affairs of men and women. This gospel of light, hope, and salvation is the basis of the Church's commission in 1 Timothy 3:5 to serve as the pillar and support of the truth in society.

The Spirit of God created the world as a perfect creation. Sin ruined this state of perfection. God created Adam and his descendants to live in perfect harmony with Him. When Adam and Eve chose to respond to Satan's lie, the power of sin corrupted their relationship with God. Adam had been created to live in perfect fellowship with God. Due to sin, he found himself alienated from God. The corrupting power of sin has affected God's creation ever since the days of Eden. The present world system is a result of that sinful leaven. The world system is an alienated system, a system organized and maintained apart from the laws of God and apart from fellowship with Him. Human society, since it is organized and maintained apart from God, ultimately becomes a society which is organized against God, a society which exists defying God's rule. Part of this rebellion is open rebellion, rebellion based upon pride and selfishness. Some of it is the result of a lack of knowledge. It is the calling of the Church to be a light in a dark world, to live and preach the gospel so that people will at least have enough facts before them to make a decision on the great issues of our time: truth versus falsehood, right versus wrong, good versus evil.

The New Testament specifically refers to God's "church" as a mystery. "Mystery" in Bible parlance refers to something which remains hidden until God is ready to reveal it. Although it had been in His plan since before the foundation of the world, God revealed the church at Pentecost. He also introduced the church age—the age in which we have been living for nearly two thousand years. The Church age ends with the Rapture of the Church. Until then, the Church has a job to do.

Now and then you see news stories on television about local high school bands who earn money to go on outings to famous places, to perform and to sightsee. They festively board their buses and head off to places like Disney World, the Rose Bowl Parade, and so forth. I am sure it is a great time for all, a memorable time. Like so many such memories, however, since there is no eternal application, it will be of no true significance. It is an example of what I might call a "good thing." It is not the "best thing." Sometimes, in fact, by concentrating on a life filled with "good things," we miss "the best things." If that is the case, in the end, all the good things won't have been good at all—at least in the light of eternity. I am thinking of a better bus trip, one that is now packing up. Let's call it the ultimate Bible bus trip. I am referring to the Rapture of the Church. That departure will be the most significant trip any living person can make. As for all trips, preparation is necessary for that one. Good intentions will do no good. Only too late, many people who find themselves in the position of the foolish virgins in Scripture will realize that they were tragically too casual about preparation for eternity. Obviously, those who never heard about this ultimate heavenly bus trip are unlikely to be in a position to make this trip. They will miss the bus. Those who miss connections on this trip will be forced to do things the hard way in a hostile environment.

In the New Testament, *church* means an assembly of "called out ones." They are called out of the world and into relationship and fellowship with God through Jesus Christ. They are also called to share God's truth with a world that is not necessarily in love with truth. God's truth, of course, is expressed in His creation, in His Word, and in His Son. The Holy Spirit uses the Word of God to open our eyes, minds, and hearts to Christ Jesus. The basis of true discipleship is to seek and find God in His Word. The Bible is a book of principles—principles which become belief patterns and actions as they are brought to life by the Holy Spirit. It is against this revelation that we are to weigh all the customs, beliefs, actions, and even the cultures of all that we see around us.

In the New Testament, the Greek word *sozo* is translated as both salvation and deliverance. Salvation and deliverance are both events which are appropriated by faith at a specific moment in time, apprehended on the basis of a true knowledge of who Jesus Christ is, what He has done, and what He will yet do and be. At the same time, salvation and deliverance are ongoing processes of faith, worked out by God in conjunction with His plan and mankind's willingness to receive it and implement it. Thus, salvation is both completed and ongoing. Many things, of course, which are paradoxes to the natural mind are open mysteries to believers. Salvation and deliverance are based upon the finished work of Jesus Christ.

We have been saved both for something and from something. We have been saved and delivered from the domain of darkness, from the power and rule of sin, and from the entangling love of the world. We have been set apart to the lordship of Christ, to righteousness, and to a heavenly calling, to citizenship in a new society. That is the message of the Church. That is also the message of the parable with which I shall end my book.

"To bring out prisoners from the dungeon, And those who dwell in darkness from the prison. I am the Lord, that is My name" (Isa. 42:7-8). "To hear the groaning of the prisoner; to set free those who were doomed to death" (Ps. 102:20). "The Lord sets the prisoners free" (Ps. 146:7). Once upon a time there were three prisoners. They were imprisoned in the deepest and darkest part of the most terrible prison which has ever existed. They were held captive by the cruelest and most powerful of jailers who has ever existed. No escape was possible. Therefore, no hope was possible. All that existed for the three suffering prisoners in this cruel house of bondage were misery, pain, and lonely groaning.

The prisoners thus sat dejectedly and silently in their cold, dark cell, day after lonely day. They exchanged neither words nor smiles, isolated in their individual suffering. They had lived this way for countless days and endless nights.

Suddenly, one certain day, things changed. The oppressive silence in their cell was shattered by a mighty shout and the tremendous, majestic sounding of a trumpet. The trumpet's peal seemed to sound and then resound again and again off the walls of their cell. The rusty locks on the massive cell door began to move. The rusty hinges cried shrilly as the door swung slowly open. The prisoners buried their faces in their hands as a sudden and powerful light pierced their darkness, striking eyes unaccustomed to the light.

As they peeked between their fingers, they could discern the form of a man who stood before them. They had no idea who this man might be, for they had never seen him before, but he was most assuredly a man of great power and authority, a man of might, valor, and royal demeanor. He produced a golden key and unlocked the chains which held them shackled to the cold wall. In a tone of authority and compassion he said,

The dark lord who has held you captive for so long has been overthrown. You are now free to go if you recognize the lordship of the One Who has overcome your jailer, and if you promise to serve Him alone. If you are indeed willing to trust and serve Him, you may come to His palace to meet this Great King. You may even dwell with Him in His palace if you elect to do so and be treated as a Prince, with all the rank, privileges, authority, and power of royalty. All you need do is to respond in obedience to the truth that you have heard.

Then suddenly he was gone as quickly as he had come. The door to their cell, however, remained open. The three men were at first too stunned to react. Slowly, they began to timidly discuss what they had seen and heard. The oldest prisoner, the one who had been there the longest, was the first to speak. He said,

I cannot go. Perhaps I have grown used to my chains. Change frightens me more than chains. This is the only life I have ever known. I cannot believe that what this man said to us is true. It is all too easy. Life is hard. Things like this don't happen. Especially to me. It must be a trick. I cannot go. I will not go. Perhaps some day I will manage to find a way of escape on my own.

And he did not go. No amount of discussion, persuasion, reasoning, or pleading could change his mind. As far as we know, he remains in that prison to this very day. Perhaps he died there. The second prisoner said, "I believe it is true. I am leaving this vile place." With that, he jumped up, shook off his chains, and ran through the open door. He ran into the nearby village. He lived out the rest of his life there in relative comfort. He did not go on to the palace because he did not know what might be expected of him there. The story

about living as a prince seemed too good to be true to
him. He knew that he could never deserve that, and he
did not wish to risk losing what he had already gained.
He decided to accept what seemed good to him, but in
so doing, he also lost out on the very best. He lived out
his life with little impact on those around him. He
hardly ever spoke to people of how he had been liber-
ated from prison. He never shared with them what he
had heard about the Great King.

The third prisoner walked slowly through the open
cell door. He also walked through the nearby village.
He walked resolutely on to the palace of the Great
King, the King of Kings. He presented himself at the
gate on the basis of the truth which he had heard in
prison and which he had believed to be true. He was
given a royal welcome. He was also given new, shining
robes to wear and a signet ring of authority, which was
placed on his finger. Thus, he was freely and warmly
welcomed into the household of the King. He lived for
the rest of his days in warm and loving fellowship with
the King Himself and with the rest of His royal family.
He loved them all more each day, and he served the
King well, loyally, fruitfully, and faithfully. It was, in
fact, his greatest joy to serve his King and to have
fellowship with Him. He was given royal authority to
go forth in the name of His King, to visit terrible
prisons, such as the one in which he had languished
for so long, and in which he had first heard the Good
News. He proclaimed the same message of freedom to
others which he himself had heard and believed. He
too blew great majestic, resounding blasts on his golden
trumpet, announcing the freedom of the truth. Those
who believed the truth he freely offered them also
went free. Truth applied brings freedom. This is the
message of the Church! He whom the Son sets free is
free indeed (John 8:31-36). It is a message that our
society needs.

Before its maiden voyage, the oceanliner Titanic was advertised as "the ship which even God couldn't sink." It was a marvel of technology and opulent comfort, a floating monument to man's ego. The crew and the backers of the Titanic proved to be both overconfident and unprepared. This lethal combination sealed the fate of the Titanic. Pride gave way to amazement, and amazement soon gave way to desperation. Once people realized that the Titanic could not be saved, the priorities of most of those aboard changed. The main concern began to be to save as many lives as possible before the ship went down by sending them to safety in the lifeboats.

Our society is like the Titanic. It has already hit the iceberg and it is taking on water. Since we cannot patch the ship up anymore, it is time to consider the best way to save as many of the passengers as possible. The job of the Church is to preach the gospel of eternal hope to those who suddenly find themselves in a life-threatening position. On the Titanic, heroic individuals ministered to the emotional and physical needs of others right up to the last second. That too is the job of the Church. Although eternity is always just a heartbeat away, many people cruise through their lives unaware and unconcerned until they hit an iceberg. When they do, only the truth can save them.

Unfortunately, life is filled with icebergs. At the end of it all, however, the most important question a person could ever consider is: "Who is Jesus Christ to you?"

A PERSONAL P.S.

On rare occasions I have written to authors whose books have touched me in some way. Generally, they didn't respond. I didn't really expect them to, but I must admit that I was a tiny bit disappointed when they didn't. On the other hand, I have always been touched when somebody who read my book took the time and went to the trouble to track me down and either write me a letter or give me a call. I have met some very interesting people that way. Ergo, I decided that I would make it easy for any of you who might read this book and feel like writing me a letter to find me. Perhaps you would like to make a comment, ask a question, or send me a bit of information that I would find informative, useful, or interesting. If that is the case, please do. I am already working on my next book. You can reach me at: Cheswick Christian Academy, 1407 Pittsburgh Street, Cheswick, Pennsylvania 15024.

Notes

Chapter One

1. Charles Colson, "The Abolition of Truth," *World*, vol. 9, no. 3 (19 February 1994): 22.

Chapter Two

1. Don Feder, "Pleas for social tolerance obscure reality," *Conservative Chronicle* (1 June 1994): 2.

2. Lynn Stanley, *Combat Ready* (Lafayette, Louisiana: Huntington House Publishers, 1994), 13.

3. Oswald Chambers, *My Utmost for His Highest* (New York, New York: Dodd, Mead and Company, 1935), 279.

4. Francis Schaeffer, *How Should We Then Live?* (Wheaton, Illinois: Crossway Books, 1976), 251.

5. Donald Wildmon, *The Home Invaders* (Wheaton, Illinois: Victor Books, 1986), 44.

Chapter Three

1. Paul Schenck, *The Extermination of Christianity* (Lafayette, Louisiana: Huntington House Publishers, 1993), ix.

2. Gary L. Bauer, "Who Counts the Most Important Things of All?" *Imprimis Magazine* (July 1994): 1.

3. David Thibodaux, *Beyond Political Correctness: Are There Limits to This Lunacy?* (Lafayette, Louisiana: Huntington House Publishers, 1994), 19.

4. George Will, "Nation in revolt against decades of liberalism," *Conservative Chronicle* (11 January 1995): 9.

5. Schenck, *The Extermination of Christianity*, 47.

6. Charles Colson, *Against the Night* (Ann Arbor, Michigan: Servant Publications [Vine Books], 1989), 11.

7. Linda Bowles, "Religious apartheid is official U.S. policy," *Conservative Chronicle* (4 January 1995): 27.

8. Charley Reese, "America surrenders its liberty," *Conservative Chronicle* (vol. 9, no. 4): 4.

9. John R. W. Stott, *Christian Counter-Culture: The Message of the Sermon on the Mount* (Downers Grove, Illinois: Intervarsity Press, 1978), 15.

10. Linda Bowles, "The first steps of a long journey home," *Conservative Chronicle* (30 November 1994): 6.

11. Thomas Sowell, "The grand vision of liberalism," *Conservative Chronicle* (9 November 1994): 1.

12. Schenck, *The Extermination of Christianity*, 33.

13. Linda Bowles, "Vast majority believe the country is off course," *Conservative Chronicle* (16 November 1994): 11.

14. Schenck, *The Extermination of Christianity*, 227.

Chapter Five

1. Tim LaHaye, *Faith of Our Founding Fathers* (Brentwood, Tennessee: Wolgemuth and Hyatt Publishers, 1987), 6.

2. Ibid., 6.

3. Thomas Sowell, "Revisionist historians create a new reality," *Conservative Chronicle* (12 January 1994): 26.

4. Joseph Sobran, "We have our own private Wacos," *Conservative Chronicle* (23 March 1994): 9.

5. Linda Bowles, "Who will protect us from the government?" *Conservative Chronicle* (5 October 1994): 7.

6. Ibid.

7. Clarence B. Carson, *The American Tradition* (Irvington-on-Hudson, New York: Foundation for Economic Education, 1964), 36.

8. Ibid., 5.

9. Joseph Sobran, "We live in a post-Constitutional America," *Conservative Chronicle* (2 February 1994): 11.

10. Samuel Francis, "What stupid rulings tell us about our rulers," *Conservative Chronicle* (14 September 1994): 6.

Chapter Six

1. Don Feder, "Cultural elite would have derided the Pilgrims," *Conservative Chronicle* (7 December 1994): 2.

2. Roy McFinnis, "The Why of History," *God's Word Publication* (13 January 1995): 2.

3. Richard Terrell, *The Resurrection of the Third Reich* (Lafayette, Louisiana: Huntington House Publishers, 1994): 62.

4. Paul Schenck, *The Extermination of Christianity* (Lafayette, Louisiana: Huntington House Publishers, 1993), 43.

Chapter Seven

1. Jean-Francois Steiner, *Treblinka* (New York, New York: New American Library, 1966), 216.

2. Ibid., 88.

3. Ibid., 130.

4. Paul Schenck, *The Extermination of Christianity* (Lafayette, Louisiana: Huntington House Publishers, 1993), 175.

5. Ruth Andreas-Friedrich, *Berlin Underground: 1938-1945* (New York, New York: Paragon House, 1947), 23.

6. Nechama Tec, *When Light Pierced the Darkness* (London, England: Oxford Press, 1986), 8.

7. Steiner, *Treblinka*, 225.

8. Elie Wiesel, *The Night Trilogy* (New York, New York: Hill and Wagner, 1972), 57.

9. Schenck, *The Extermination of Christianity*, 37.

10. Ibid., 26.

11. Charles Colson, *Against the Night* (Ann Arbor, Michigan: Servant Publications [Vine Books], 1989), 37, 39, 42.

12. Robert Moeller, "Dropping the 'H-Bomb'," *World*, vol. 9, no. 21 (4 June 1944): 26.

13. Ibid.

Chapter Nine

1. Pat Buchanan, "The culture war in Lake County," *Conservative Chronicle* (1 June 1994): 1.

2. Oswald Chambers, *My Utmost for His Highest* (New York, New York: Dodd, Mead and Company, 1935), 288, 267.

Chapter Ten

1. Francis A. Schaeffer, *How Should We Then Live?* (Wheaton, Illinois: Crossway Books, 1976), 227.

2. Ibid., 248.

3. Ibid., 246.

4. Samantha Smith, *Goddess Earth* (Lafayette, Louisiana: Huntington House Publishers, 1994), 51.

5. Ibid., 113.

6. Don Feder, "Cult of self-esteem dominates education," *Conservative Chronicle* (26 October 1994): 30.

7. Linda Chavez, "Pilgrims as bad guys? Come on!" *USA Today* (23 November 1994): 15A.

Chapter Eleven

1. Charley Reese, "Censorship, American style," *Conservative Chronicle* (26 October 1994): 23.

2. Paul Schenck, *The Extermination of Christianity* (Lafayette, Louisiana: Huntington House Publishers, 1993), xvii.

Chapter Thirteen

1. Tim LaHaye, *The Faith of Our Founding Fathers* (Brentwood, Tennessee: Wolgemuth and Hyatt Publishers, 1987), 64.

2. Rus Walters, *One Nation Under God*, (Washington, D.C.: Third Century Publishers, 1975), 23.

3. LaHaye, *The Faith of Our Founding Fathers*, 64-65.

4. Ibid., 52.

5. Linda Bowles, "The first steps of the long journey home," *Conservative Chronicle* (30 November 1994): 21.

6. Joseph Sobran, "Washington plays down the 10th Amendment," *Conservative Chronicle* (20 July 1994): 11.

7. Joseph Sobran, "We live in a post-Constitutional America," *Conservative Chronicle* (2 February 1994): 11.

8. Walter Williams, "Recovering liberties taken from us," *Conservative Chronicle* (7 January 1995): 25.

9. William T. Still, *New World Order: The Ancient Plan of Secret Societies* (Lafayette, Louisiana: Huntington House Publishers, 1990), 15.

10. Linda Bowles, "Who will protect us from the government?" *Conservative Chronicle* (5 October 1994): 7.

Chapter Fourteen

1. Jeffrey Hart, "Liberal ideas have collided with reality," *Conservative Chronicle* (30 November 1994): 21.

2. Cal Thomas, "Judicial rights hurt minorities," *Conservative Chronicle* (1 June 1994): 30.

3. Charley Reese, "The boundaries of abortion," *Conservative Chronicle* (21 December 1994): 16.

4. Robert Novak, "California demands action on immigration," *Conservative Chronicle* (21 December 1994): 9.

5. Pat Buchanan, "America: Wimp of the Western Hemisphere," *Conservative Chronicle* (28 December 1994): 19.

6. Samuel Francis, "Real Americans vs. the real elite in California," *Conservative Chronicle* (9 November 1994): 9.

7. Edward Grimsley, "Independence Day alarms politically correct," *Conservative Chronicle* (28 November 1994): 11.

8. Paul Harvey, "The new breed of immigrants," *Conservative Chronicle* (14 January 1995): 30.

9. Tony Snow, "Right to privacy covers only sex and abortion," *Conservative Chronicle* (21 December 1994): 19.

Chapter Fifteen

1. Walter Williams, "Education system is destroying our children," *Conservative Chronicle* (24 December 1994): 7.

2. Cal Thomas, "Abdication of the condom queen," *Conservative Chronicle* (21 December 1994): 4.

3. Don Feder, "Teen murder and the poverty of values," *Conservative Chronicle* (2 November 1994): 27.

4. Charles Colson, *Against the Night* (Ann Arbor, Michigan: Servant Publications [Vine Books], 1989), 11.

5. Charles Colson, *The Struggle for Men's Hearts and Minds* (Wheaton, Illinois: Victor Books, 1983), 12.

6. Charles Colson, "Juvenile crime," *Conservative Chronicle* (10 August 1994): 20.

Chapter Eighteen

1. William F. Buckley, "Women's movement is in the hands of fanatics," *Conservative Chronicle* (21 November 1994): 22.

2 Keith A. Fournier, "Putting a stop to America's imperial judiciary," American Center for Law and Justice tract (Virginia Beach, Virginia, 1995).

3. Ronald Reagan, *Abortion and The Conscience of the Nation* (Nashville, Tennessee: Thomas Nelson Publishers, 1984), 25.

4. Charles Colson, *The Struggle for Men's Hearts and Minds* (Wheaton, Illinois: Victor Books, 1983), 12.

5. Cal Thomas, *Book Burning* (Westchester, Illinois: Crossway Books, 1983), 41.

6. Ronald Reagan, *Abortion and The Conscience of the Nation*, 8.

7. Ibid., 12.

8. Author unknown, Heritage House tract, Snowflake, Arizona.

9. David Thibodaux, *Beyond Political Correctness: Are There Limits to This Lunacy?* (Lafayette, Louisiana: Huntington House Publishers, 1994), 130.

Chapter Nineteen

1. Francis A. Schaeffer, *The Great Evangelical Disaster* (Westchester: Crossway Books, 1984), 32-33.

Chapter Twenty

1. Scott M. Huse, *The Collapse of Evolution*, (Grand Rapids, Michigan: Baker Book House, 1983), 6.

2. Paul Schenck, *The Extermination of Christianity* (Lafayette, Louisiana: Huntington House Publishers, 1993), 152.

3. Scott M. Huse, *The Collapse of Evolution*, i, 5.

More Good Books from Huntington House

Combat Ready
How to Fight the Culture War
by Lynn Stanley

The culture war between traditional values and secular humanism is escalating. At stake are our children. The schools, the liberal media, and even the government, through Outcome Based Education, are indoctrinating our children with moral relativism, instead of moral principles. *Combat Ready* not only discloses the extent to which our society has been influenced by this "anything goes" mentality. It offers sound advice about how parents can protect their children and restore our culture to its biblical foundation.

ISBN 1-56384-074-X $9.99

A Jewish Conservative
Looks at Pagan America
by Don Feder

With eloquence and insight that rival essayists of antiquity, Don Feder's pen finds his targets in the enemies of God, family, and American tradition and morality. Deftly . . . delightfully . . . the master allegorist and Titian with a typewriter brings clarity to the most complex sociological issues and invokes giggles and wry smiles from both followers and foes. Feder is Jewish to the core, and he finds in his Judaism no inconsistency with an American Judeo-Christian ethic. Questions of morality plague school administrators, district court judges, senators, congressmen, parents, and employers; they are wrestling for answers in a "changing world." Feder challenges this generation and directs inquirers to the original books of wisdom: the Torah and the Bible.

ISBN 1-56384-036-7 Trade Paper $9.99
ISBN 1-56384-037-5 Hardcover $19.99

Order These Huntington House Books !

- America Betrayed—Marlin Maddoux. 7.99
- The Assault—Dale A. Berryhill 9.99
- Beyond Political Correctness—David Thibodaux 9.99
- The Best of Human Events—Edited by James C. Roberts 34.95
- Bleeding Hearts and Propaganda—James R. Spencer 9.99
- Can Families Survive in Pagan America?—Samuel Dresner 15.99
- Circle of Death—Richmond Odom 10.99
- Combat Ready—Lynn Stanley 9.99
- Conservative, American & Jewish—Jacob Neusner 9.99
- The Dark Side of Freemasonry—Ed Decker 9.99
- The Demonic Roots of Globalism—Gary Kah 10.99
- Don't Touch That Dial—Barbara Hattemer & Robert Showers . . . . . 9.99/19.99 HB
- En Route to Global Occupation—Gary Kah 9.99
- Everyday Evangelism—Ray Comfort 10.99
- *Exposing the AIDS Scandal—Dr. Paul Cameron 7.99/2.99
- Freud's War with God—Jack Wright, Jr. 7.99
- Gays & Guns—John Eidsmoe . . . . 7.99/14.99 HB
- Global Bondage—Cliff Kincaid 10.99
- Goddess Earth—Samantha Smith 9.99
- Health Begins in Him—Terry Dorian 9.99
- Heresy Hunters—Jim Spencer 8.99
- Hidden Dangers of the Rainbow—Constance Cumbey 9.99
- High-Voltage Christianity—Michael Brown 10.99
- High on Adventure—Stephen Arrington 8.99
- Homeless in America—Jeremy Reynalds 9.99
- How to Homeschool (Yes, You!)—Julia Toto 3.99
- Hungry for God—Larry E. Myers 9.99
- I Shot an Elephant in My Pajamas—Morrie Ryskind w/ John Roberts 12.99
- *Inside the New Age Nightmare—Randall Baer 9.99/2.99
- A Jewish Conservative Looks at Pagan America—Don Feder . . . . . 9.99/19.99 HB
- Journey into Darkness—Stephen Arrington 9.99
- Kinsey, Sex and Fraud—Dr. Judith A. Reisman & Edward Eichel 11.99
- The Liberal Contradiction—Dale A. Berryhill 9.99
- Legalized Gambling—John Eidsmoe 7.99
- Loyal Opposition—John Eidsmoe 8.99
- The Media Hates Conservatives—Dale A. Berryhill . . . . 9.99/19.99 HB
- New Gods for a New Age—Richmond Odom 9.99
- One Man, One Woman, One Lifetime—Rabbi Reuven Bulka 7.99
- Out of Control—Brenda Scott . . . . 9.99/19.99 HB
- Outcome-Based Education—Peg Luksik & Pamela Hoffecker 9.99
- The Parched Soul of America—Leslie Kay Hedger w/ Dave Reagan 10.99
- Please Tell Me—Tom McKenney 9.99
- Political Correctness—David Thibodaux 9.99
- Resurrecting the Third Reich—Richard Terrell 9.99
- Revival: Its Principles and Personalities—Winkie Pratney 10.99

Available in Salt Series

Available at bookstores everywhere or order direct from:
Huntington House Publishers • P.O. Box 53788 • Lafayette, LA 70505
Send check/money order. For faster service use VISA/MASTERCARD.
Call toll-free 1-800-749-4009.
Add: Freight and handling, $3.50 for the first book ordered, and $.50 for
each additional book up to 5 books.